Drive Yourself Sane

Using the Uncommon Sense of General Semantics

Third Edition

Susan Presby Kodish
and
Bruce I. Kodish

Foreword by Albert Ellis

Pasadena, CA

Drive Yourself Sane: Using The Uncommon Sense of General Semantics. Third Edition
by Susan Presby Kodish and Bruce I. Kodish
Copyright © 2011 by Susan Presby Kodish and Bruce I. Kodish

Published by Extensional Publishing
                Email: ExtensionalPubl@aol.com

Publisher's Catalogue in Publication Data
Kodish, Susan Presby and Kodish, Bruce I.
Drive Yourself Sane: Using The Uncommon Sense of General Semantics. Third Edition / by Susan Presby Kodish and Bruce I. Kodish
Pasadena, CA: Extensional Publishing, © 2011
242 pp. includes index
ISBN 978-0-9700664-1-1 (paperback: acid free paper)
Library of Congress Control Number: 2010935520

1. General Semantics 2. Meaning (Psychology) 2. Applied Epistemology 3. Thinking Skills 4. Communication 5. I. Title. II. Kodish, Susan Presby. III. Kodish, Bruce I.

LC Classification # B820
Dewey Decimal Classification # 149/.94 21

Cover Design by Bruce Kodish
Illustrations/Drawings on pages 28, 53, 65, 66, 69, 78, 107 by Rebecca Butcher Schoenfliess; on pages 26, 34, 36, 61, 91, 202 used with permission of the Alfred Korzybski estate; on page 164 used with permission of W.B.Saunders Co. from the book *Atlas of Human Anatomy* by Dr. Barry J. Anson.

For more information, including how to contact GS organizations, go to www.driveyourselfsane.com
You may contact the authors at DriveSelfSane@aol.com

...a young mathematician, [attending a general-semantics seminar]... came dashing in one morning and started hollering, "General semantics, general semantics, is driving me sane!"

...You take a point of view whether you like it or not. You cannot fail to take a point of view, and the question becomes whether the point of view you're taking is an anachronism. Is it 19th century, 18th century, or 17th century, or the 20th century? Is it now? So there is a responsibility that we have for ourselves.

Harry Holtzman[1]

Contents

List of Figures   10

Preface to the Third Edition   11

Preface to the Second Edition   12

Acknowledgments   13

Foreword by Albert Ellis, PhD   14

On Reading This Book   16

1. Introductions   17
An introduction to the authors and to general semantics.

2. Glass Doors and Unicorns   22
How we acquire and talk about information, and how this relates to how we behave. How we use language to learn from our own and others' experiences and, through this, can improve our lives.

    The General-Semantics System   23

    How Your Experience Works   24

    What Makes Humans Human?   27

    Applications   29

3. Uncommon Sense   30
The role of assumptions in our lives and how to examine and revise them. Doing this, by applying a scientific attitude in our daily lives, leads to uncommon sense.

    Examining Assumptions   31

    Logical Fate   33

    Scientific Method   35

    World Views   37

    Lateral Thinking   38

    Applying a Scientific Attitude   40

    Tentative Forever   41

    Applications   43

4. Endless Complexities 45
Internal and external influences on how we function and create 'meanings'. These influences include our language environments.

Evaluational (Semantic) Transactions	46
The Organism-as-a-Whole-in-Environments	47
Landscapes of 'Meaning'	48
Internal Landscapes	50
External Landscapes	52
Applications	56

5. The Process of Abstracting 59
How we, as observers, construct our observations. The importance of recognizing how perceptions are influenced by expectations, and are more and less reliable.

Our Process World	60
The Observer-Observed Continuum	62
Our Nervous Systems	63
Abstracting	67
Perceiving	70
Applications	73

6. Mapping Structures 74
The role of the maps we create of the territories of our lives. How to usefully increase our awareness of them, and of how things are related.

Structure and Knowledge	75
Mapping	76
Functional Functioning	79
Non-Additivity	83
Consciousness of Mapping	86
Applications	87

7. The Structural Differential   89
*Becoming more aware of levels involved in forming perceptions
and talking about them. Importance of differentiating among
these levels, in order to more effectively deal with what's
going on.*
Levels of Abstracting   90
Identification   95
'Natural' (Appropriate) Order of Abstracting   98
Applications   99

8. Non-Verbal Awareness   100
*How to allow silent contemplation, noting its effects on
overall functioning and aesthetic appreciation. Improving
communications by developing an ability to get quiet inside.*
Turning Down the Volume   101
Contemplating   102
Semantic (Evaluational) Relaxation   104
Sensory Awareness   104
The Means Whereby   108
Challenging Assumptions Non-Verbally   109
Applications   111

9. Verbal Awareness   112
*How to distinguish facts from inferences and determine the
degree of truth in a situation. When and how to seek more
information in order to make better sense of things.*
In the Dark   113
Facts and Inferences   114
Fact-Inference Continuum   116
Converging Inferences   117
Observations-Descriptions-Facts-Inferences   119
What We Can Determine: Degrees of Probability   121
More about Less, Less about More   124
Applications   125

10. The Structure of Language 127
Some aspects of everyday language which influence our perceptions and understandings. Introducing some ways to use language more effectively.

The Aristotelian Orientation 130
A Non-Aristotelian Orientation 132
Non-Identity 134
Non-Elementalism 135
The "Ises" 136
Non-Allness 139
Either/Or 139
Causation 141
Labeling 142
Applications 144

11. Self-Reflexive Mapping 146
How to make sense with words that have multiple 'meanings'. Problems involved with our ability to think about our thinking and react to our reactions; ways to solve them.

Multi-'Meaning' 147
Multiordinality 149
Reacting to Our Reactions 151
Open Systems 153
Applications 155

12. The Extensional Orientation 157
Distinguishing fact-based approaches, as compared with definition-based approaches. Advantages and methods of a 'fact'-based approach.

Intensional and Extensional 'Meanings' 158
Intensional and Extensional Orientations 160
Applications 166

13. Getting Extensional   167

Techniques for delaying automatic behavior and increasing the probability of acting appropriately in each situation. Specific language modifications that can improve communications and relationships.

Delayed Evaluating   169
Extensional Devices   170
  Indexing   170
  Dating   173
  Et Cetera (Etc.)   174
  Quotes and Hyphens   174
Other Extensional Techniques   175
  Visualization   176
  Non-Allness Terms   176
  Qualifying and Quantifying   177
  One Step at a Time   178
  English without "Ises" (E-Prime)   179
  English Minus Absolutisms (EMA)   180
Overcoming IFD Disease   181
Questioning Questions   182
Applications   183

14. Time-Binding   186

A review of general semantics, focusing on how to develop a positive future for individuals and society. Special attention to communications and relationships.

Taking Responsibility   188
Cooperating   190
Communicating   192
Personal Time-Binding   197
Applications   198

15. Et Cetera 199
How to continue learning and using general semantics
to avoid and solve problems and enjoy life more.
   Applications 201

On Alfred Korzybski 202
A brief history of his life and work. Korzybski: A Biography
provides a comprehensive history.

What Did Alfred Want? 206
"What does he or she want?" seems to us one of the most
important questions for understanding anyone's life. What did
Korzybski want? What was he aiming for? What difference
does it make to you?

Glossary 212

Notes 218

Bibliography 228

Index 234

About the Authors 242

List of Figures

2-1 The Structural Differential   26

3-1 Logical Fate   34

3-2 Revising Assumptions   36

4-1 Organism-as-a-Whole-in-an-Environment   53

5-1 Change Thinging   61

5-2 The Human Nervous System   65

5-3 Nerve Cells and Synapses   66

5-4 The Process of Abstracting   69

5-5 Duck-Rabbit   70

5-6 'Impossible'   71

6-1 A Functional Curve   82

6-2 An Additive, Linear Function   84

6-3 A Non-Additive, Non-Linear Function   85

7-1 The Structural Differential   91

9-1 Fact-Inference Continuum   116

12-1 Stomach – Variations in Form   164

Preface to the Third Edition

In 1992 Charlotte Schuchardt Read, Alfred Korzybski's confidential secretary and literary executor, suggested that we write an introductory book on general semantics—but one with a difference. Previous introductions had mainly treated general semantics (GS) from the perspective of speech and language studies or psychology. Some misrepresented Korzybski's work and/or presented it in a fragmentary manner. Missing was a *brief* and *reliable* treatment of Korzybski's work as a whole, in its own right *as a system*. Thus was born the first edition of *Drive Yourself Sane*, published in 1993 by the Institute of General Semantics. Having gone through two editions and numerous reprintings, the book has continued to fulfill the needs and desires of readers for a dependable introduction to *korzybskian general semantics*. As we prepare this Third Edition, we reflect on many changes.

Foremost for us have been the deaths of most of our teachers, mentors and colleagues from the Institute's post-Korzybski but still quite korzybskian heyday in the last half of the 20th Century. Of those whom we acknowledged in previous editions, Dorothy Berleth, Helen Hafner, Ken Johnson, Stuart Mayper, Tom Nelson, Bob Pula, Charlotte Schuchardt Read, Allen Walker Read and Ralph Wesselmann are no longer with us. Marjorie Zelner, the Institute's Administrator for almost two decades and our friend, tragically died in 2000 before her 50th birthday. Our friend, GS teacher Bernie Kahane, who helped edit the book, and Susan's mentor, psychologist and REBT founder Albert Ellis, who wrote the Foreword, also died. Gone too is our dear friend Homer Jean Moore, Jr.—an extraordinary korzybskian scholar and GS "student-practitioner" (his own designation even though he taught advanced classes), who inspired us with his unstinting helpfulness and humor. Fortunately, Milton Dawes, master scholar-practitioner-teacher of korzybskian GS, remains a close friend and sounding board.

In considering the lineage of Korzybski's work, we note that, of those named above, Charlotte, Allen and Helen personally studied closely with Korzybski. We studied with them, with some of Korzybski's other students and his students' students, and in turn became teachers. As the now-older generation in the korzybskian tradition, we increasingly consider ourselves responsible for doing what we can to bring to others Korzybski's system of personal education for living. Thus this Third Edition, published in conjunction with the forthcoming *Korzybski: A Biography*, by Bruce. We have made some revisions throughout the text and have added a supplemental chapter, "What Did Alfred Want?" which we believe provides additional vital background for understanding Korzybski's aims, as well as our own.

Nothing Never Happens, as Ken Johnson aptly named one of his books. Personal, local, regional, national and international events, including technological innovations, bring moment-to-moment changes for better and worse—not surprising, but suggesting that the wisest course for us is to stay in touch and adapt. Wise, but not easy. This book provides time-tested methods for making the most of the primary tools we have for effectively adapting to change, tools we were born with: our brain-nervous systems with their marvelous capacities to learn from and build upon our own and other people's experiences. We wish you well in the on-going process of sharpening your tools.
— Susan and Bruce Kodish, August 2010

Preface to the Second Edition

We thank readers of the First Edition for their many gratifying positive reactions and for comments leading to revisions. As readers ourselves, we also found room for some improvements and places where we wanted to update what we had written. We welcome the first time reader as well as anyone returning for review and to read what's new. We hope that this Second Edition will provide both with new perspectives on how to develop uncommon sense.

Acknowledgments

We thank Dorothy R. Berleth, Milton Dawes, Dr. Helen Hafner, Dr. Kenneth G. Johnson, Dr. Stuart A. Mayper, Thomas E. Nelson, Robert P. Pula, Charlotte Schuchardt Read, Dr. Allen Walker Read, Ralph Wesselmann: fine, inspiring teachers who have become wonderful friends. Their influence permeates this book. We thank Milton Dawes, Dr. Albert Ellis, Bernie Kahane, Marilyn Kodish, Dr. Stuart A. Mayper, Jeffrey Mordkowitz, David Presby, Dr. Joan Presby, Robert P. Pula, Charlotte Schuchardt Read, and Dr. Joan Sophie for reading the book-in-progress and making helpful suggestions. We thank Milton Dawes for help in preparing the Index and Marjorie Zelner for her help in producing the first edition. Homer J. Moore, Jr. provided valuable input for the Second Edition. We thank Ben Hauck for his help in proofreading the Third Edition.

We thank each other for forbearance and the joy of creative collaboration.

Foreword (1993)

I am delighted to see Susan and Bruce Kodish's *Drive Yourself Sane: Using the Uncommon Sense of General Semantics* in print because, like Wendell Johnson's *People in Quandaries*, it applies Alfred Korzybski's brilliant general-semantics philosophy to its readers' everyday lives and shows them how to live more sanely in a still highly irrational and partially insane world. As Korzybski showed, and as this book demonstrates again – but in much clearer and down-to-earth language than that often used by the founder of general semantics – almost all of us humans *easily* and *naturally* identify our *self* with our *behavior*, define ourselves as *good* or *bad people*, overgeneralize, and speak and think self-defeatingly and world-defeatingly. And, as the authors markedly point out, we can train ourselves to do so considerably less often and less intensely.

Rational Emotive Behavior Therapy (REBT), the pioneering form of cognitive-behavior therapy that I originated in 1955 and that has been quite popular since that time, significantly overlaps with general semantics, as I showed in detail in my Alfred Korzybski Memorial Lecture in New York in 1991. This is hardly a coincidence, because I read Stuart Chase's *The Tyranny of Words* (New York: Harcourt Brace, 1938) and S. I. Hayakawa's *Language in Action* (New York: Harcourt Brace, 1943) in the 1940s. In the 1950s, I finally read Korzybski's *Science and Sanity* (Englewood, NJ: International Non-Aristotelian Publishing Company, 1933, 1958) and his essay, "The Role of Language in the Perceptual Processes" in Robert R. Blake and Glenn V. Ramsey, *Perception: An Approach to Personality* (New York: Ronald, 1951); and I cited him a number of times in my articles on REBT and in my books, *A Guide to Rational Living* (Englewood Cliffs, NJ: 1961) and *Reason and Emotion in Psychotherapy* (Secaucus, NJ: Citadel, 1962).

I learned about D. David Bourland's advocacy of E-Prime in 1969 and, encouraged by one of our main Rational Emotive Behavior therapists, Dr. Robert Moore, I began writing a number of articles and books in E-Prime, including the first popular books written in this general-semantics oriented kind of language, *How To Live With A "Neurotic"* (North Hollywood, CA: Wilshire, 1975), *A New Guide To Rational Living* (North Hollywood, CA: Wilshire, 1975), *Anger-How To Live With It and Without It* (Secaucus, NJ: Citadel, 1977), and *Overcoming Procrastination* (New York: New American Library, 1977).

REBT and general semantics particularly go together because both disclose and actively dispute people's absolutist, one-sided, rigid, musturbatory thinking. As Susan and Bruce Kodish point out, Rational Emotive Behavior Therapy shows people their dogmatic, either/or, inflexible shoulds, oughts, and musts, and also shows them a number of cognitive, emotive and behavioral methods to reduce their self-defeating thoughts, feelings, and behaviors. The useful applications and exercises that the authors include at the end of each chapter overlap with many of the homework assignments that REBT practitioners – including Susan herself – work out in collaboration with their clients to minimize their emotional disturbances and their non-self-actualizing behaviors.

Readers who carefully read this book and who work at using the valuable aspects of general semantics that Susan and Bruce beautifully explain don't *have* to drive themselves sane. But they *probably* will!

Albert Ellis, Ph.D.

On Reading This Book

General Semantics presents an uncommon approach to living. We believe its value lies in its differentness. Acquiring this different approach can help us avoid and solve problems better, and improve how we relate and communicate. Using this approach we can go beyond problem-solving to find new opportunities to enhance our lives.

On the surface, much of what we say may seem 'simple', even 'obvious'. As you read, you may find the 'obvious' becoming more complex; the 'simple' not easy to understand and even less easy to apply. While we have worked to present some very complex notions in as understandable a way as possible, at times you may feel confused in the process of getting it.

At times we present these notions in uncommon ways. We draw your attention to one of those ways here, in order to reduce or avoid some confusion. We use single quotes, not only in their standard usage to indicate a quote within a quote, but also to sometimes mark off terms and phrases requiring caution for a variety of reasons from a general-semantics perspective. For example, in the preceding paragraph, we put "obvious" and "simple" in single quotes in order to suggest that these terms be interpreted with care, since they may misrepresent situations to which they are applied. We also occasionally use single quotes to indicate playful and metaphorical terms and phrases.

We have included a glossary of terms. Terms defined in the Glossary are written in SMALL CAPS the first time they appear in the text.

In reading this book, we suggest that you welcome some initial confusion as an indication that you are acquiring a new way of approaching old problems. As the 'strange' becomes familiar, you can benefit from general semantics as we have. We suggest you follow the advice of an old maxim: "When in perplexity, read on."[2] And remember, words are not enough.

Chapter 1

Introductions

GENERAL SEMANTICS (sometimes referred to as GS) was developed by Alfred Korzybski, a Polish engineer who settled in the United States following World War I. He was appalled by the massive war destruction and determined to answer the question of how humans so successfully advance technologically yet make such a mess of their general human affairs. From his more than ten-year study of this question, he formulated general semantics, most fully presented in his book *Science and Sanity* (1933).

General semantics provides the basis for Susan's work as a psychologist and Bruce's work as a physical therapist practicing posture-movement therapy and education. As part of our general-semantics orientation, we recognize that what we write here necessarily reflects our own unique understandings of this orientation. Therefore, we want to start this book by introducing ourselves to you.

Susan: My first counseling supervisor pulled *People in Quandaries*, Wendell Johnson's classic GS popularization, from his bookshelf. "You should read this book because you're already working this way", he said, after he listened to a tape of my work during my doctoral training in psychology. Thus began my experiences with GS.

Subsequent study and use of Rational Emotive Behavior Therapy (REBT), a therapy in part derived from GS, encouraged me to pursue these experiences further. After attending two Institute of General Semantics (IGS) seminar-workshops, I joined the teaching staff in 1983, continuing that work until 1997. As Education Director of the Institute, a senior editor of the *General Semantics Bulletin,* editor-in-chief of the IGS newsletter *Time-Bindings,* and through writing and presenting general semantics, I deepened my knowledge and ability to apply general semantics in a variety of situations.

I've found these experiences so useful and deeply satisfying, both professionally and personally, that I want others to have the benefits that such experiences can bring.

What kinds of benefits? I well remember my first GS seminar. Among other things, I felt impressed by the staff, and some others there, who had studied and worked to apply GS over many years. I found them particularly warm, caring and careful, attentive, and concerned with others and the world around them. I learned that they also achieved professionally at a high level. As I continued my work in this discipline, I learned that when we use GS we are likely to get similar results.

Bruce: As a bookish teenager, I found *The Tyranny of Words,* by Stuart Chase, on a magazine's suggested reading list for young people. Something about the title got my attention. After reading that book, I wanted more and started reading other books about general semantics. A turning point came when I happened upon *People in Quandaries* in my junior high school library. It seemed like one of the strangest books I had ever read. I felt amazed that somebody actually thought like that. I wanted more of this strangeness, because it made so much more sense to me than other things I heard and read.

As I continued my reading, I found I could use this approach to help myself. I followed a trail from there to the International Society for General Semantics; the Society's journal, *ETC.*; *Science and Sanity*; the Institute of General Semantics; and the Institute's seminar-workshops.

As I studied physical therapy and posture-movement education, I found that having GS as an orientation helped me to learn well and to solve problems effectively. This encouraged me to deepen my involvement in this work.

I served as administrator of Institute seminar-workshops, on the teaching staff, as a senior editor of the *General Semantics Bulletin,* and production editor of *Time-Bindings.* As both chairman and member of the IGS publications committee, I oversaw and contributed to the production of a number of important books including the Fifth Edition of *Science and Sanity.* I now write about and present GS in a variety of forums. My doctorate is in Applied Epistemology: General Semantics.[3]

Susan and Bruce: Having met at a GS seminar-workshop, we have continued together to develop our study and application of this discipline. In our individual practices of psychotherapy and posture-movement therapy and education, and in workshops, we apply GS to help people improve the way they manage their lives.

Using GS, we recognize the importance of focusing on each person's unique experiences, closely observing each person's functioning. We also recognize that in order for people to learn from their experience, they need an understanding of how their experience works. How can people best EVALUATE their experiences? How can they go beyond what they already know? As Susan's father said, "The problem with learning from experience is that you never have exactly the same experience twice." How do we best prepare for whatever new occurs "the next time"? In GS we find guidelines for answering these important questions.

Because we work so closely together and share similar views, and have collaborated so intensely on the production of this book, we use "we" rather than "I" for the most part in referring to ourselves. We use our individual names in telling stories which relate specifically to one of us.

We find that using GS helps us to relate well. We find that when we disagree, even heatedly (and that happens), using the methods we describe in this book helps us to resolve issues quickly and avoid damage to our relationship. Using it consistently enriches our relationship with humor and depth of understanding.

You too can function better in your life by using GS. You can learn how to improve the way you evaluate, so that you can make more full use of your potentialities, learn more easily, cope better with uncertainty and change, achieve more of what you want and avoid more of what you don't want.

While we don't view GS as a substitute for therapy, using it can create broad therapeutic effects in helping you to solve problems and to relate and communicate well. Preventively, using it can help you to avoid problems and to create greater opportunities.

Many people apply it in their professional lives, as well as use it to improve their day-to-day activities and relationships. Teachers, health professionals, psychologists, business people, engineers, computer specialists, artists, lawyers and others find it of great value in helping resolve individual, organizational and global problems.

If you ever find yourself in muddles and wonder how you and others can extricate yourselves from them, if you would like to avoid and solve problems better, then read on.

Applications

What issue(s), problem(s), question(s) would you like to work on using general semantics? Writing these down can make applying GS more useful for you. Therefore, we suggest that you keep a journal as you read this book. Each day or week you can write down your own discoveries about the points made in each chapter as they relate to your concerns. You can also relate these points to what you observe in your own and others' evaluating and in your other reading.

At the end of each chapter we list experiments and questions related to the chapter. These can be worked on individually and/or with others and serve as a summary of the main points of the chapter.

Chapter 2

Glass Doors and Unicorns

Learning may be defined as a relatively permanent change in behavior that occurs as the result of prior experience... *Learning could be defined more simply as "profiting from experience," were it not that some learning does not "profit" the learner; useless and harmful habits are learned just as useful ones are.*

Ernest R. Hilgard, et. al.[4]

Most, not all, of the details of this general theory are vaguely known; it seems that the main novelty consists in the building up of an autonomous system.

Alfred Korzybski[5]

In a restaurant one day, we noticed a woman having a cup of tea. She used a spoon to stir in some sugar and then left the spoon in her cup. As she lifted the cup to drink, the spoon handle poked her in the eye. Each time she sipped, she left the spoon in her cup and continued poking herself in the eye. Now perhaps the woman enjoyed doing this to herself. We suspect not, and she could have injured her eye. Failing to learn, or "profit", from her experience, stuck in her behavior, she was not evaluating her situation adequately in order to solve a problem.

In what ways do you "poke yourself in the eye"? How adequately do you evaluate? Using the system of general semantics, you can learn how to learn from your experience by learning about how your experience works.

The General-Semantics System

Korzybski chose "general semantics" as the unitary term (although it consists of two words) for his general theory of EVALUATION to maintain historical continuity with related studies, yet indicate his focus on larger issues of 'meanings' beyond the verbal.* As he pointed out in numerous published works, public lectures, etc., Korzybski used the word 'semantic' in relation to his own work as a modifying term synonymous with 'evaluation(al)'. However, subsequently many people confused "general semantics" with "semantics," i.e., more narrow-focused philosophical or linguistic approaches to 'meaning'. For example, when we're interested in the word "unicorn"—what dictionaries say it 'means', its history of 'meanings'and what it might refer to—we are involved with "semantics".

General semantics (which we'll abreviate whenever possible as GS) involves much broader issues. Using GS, we're concerned with understanding how we evaluate, with the non-verbal, inner life of each individual, with how each of us experiences and makes sense of our experiences, including how we use language and how language 'uses' us. While we're interested in what the word "unicorn" refers to and how a dictionary might define it, we have more interest in the person using the word, with the kind of evaluating that might lead people to look for unicorns in their back yards. Do they think that they have found some? Do they re-evaluate their search when they don't find any? Do they investigate how they came to be looking for unicorns? How are they experiencing the search? How do they talk about it? How are they experiencing the process of evaluating what has happened? How do they know what they say they know?

GS involves an interrelated set of elements, which, taken together, can help us answer these and similar questions. We

---

* When using the term as a modifier, as in "the general-semantics system," we follow standard practice by connecting the term's two parts with a hyphen.

take into consideration what is happening in the world around and in us, how we get our information about those happenings, how we talk about such information, and how we behave.

Each of the elements in the general-semantics system influences and depends on the others. In presenting these elements to you, we necessarily talk about some before we talk about others, yet to understand those we discuss first, you may wish you already knew about what comes later.

To a certain extent, this situation mirrors the stories of our lives. We function with incomplete information and do our best by making the most of what we have. The advantage of reading a book lies in our ability to do it again. So as you're reading this book, don't worry if and when you feel confused. As you read on, you'll find that we repeat certain points in greater detail and with more examples. You can then reread as necessary. In the process, you can create within yourself the system of GS in a way that you can use it best.

How Your Experience Works

What do we intend when we talk about how your experience works? Korzybski developed a model, which he called the STRUCTURAL DIFFERENTIAL,[6] to represent our experiencing process. (Refer to Figure 2-1 on page 26.) We will be returning to this model and process in greater detail later. However, we introduce them here in order to provide you with a framework for what follows.

According to the best current scientific knowledge, we and everything else are composed of configurations of very tiny 'processes', so tiny that we can't even see them with a microscope. From the whirl of activity of these 'processes', we perceive and create our sense of what is happening in and around us. We call this whirl the EVENT (PROCESS) LEVEL.

From the event, each of us perceives differently and so creates a different experience. At this perceiving level, we sense but have no words for our experiences. You have probably had the experience of "knowing" something and yet feeling unable to convey this to someone else adequately; you may say, "It's hard to put into words", at such times. We call this the silent, OBJECT LEVEL.

Yet we do put many things into words, and this ability represents a central difference between us and other forms of life. We can use language; we can operate at VERBAL LEVELS.

As an example, let's talk about apples. Imagine an apple on your kitchen counter.

From childhood, we learn to label and describe what we perceive. We learn, for example, that this thing we can point to, touch and eat is *called* an apple. We can call this use of language the DESCRIPTIVE LEVEL, or the level of statements of 'facts'.

We also learn to make inferences about our experiences. In learning that what we call an apple tastes good, we infer that when we see something else that looks like what we call an apple, this something else will taste good too. We call this INFERENCE LEVEL$_1$. We generalize that certain things shaped similarly but looking somewhat different are all called apples. We form "theories"; for example, the theory that anything we see which looks like what we've learned to call an apple will also taste good. Based on such predictions, we may take a bite out of a plastic "apple" or a rotting one. We call this INFERENCE LEVEL$_2$.

We can talk about each of these levels of experience, and then talk about our talking, make inferences about our inferences, etc. Theoretically, this process can go on unendingly. So we say, ET CETERA (ETC.).

When we function at our best, we use our ability to evaluate in this way to lead us back to events and our silent-level experiences and observations of them. This helps us to eat apples we find delicious and avoid eating the rotten or plastic ones.

These different levels occur together. However, we often are not aware of them or of how they affect our lives. Using GS we focus our attention on them, and separate out the different levels in order to understand them better and function more effectively.

You may feel curious about what you see in the structural differential model that we haven't discussed yet (and peek ahead to Chapter 7, if you feel like you can't wait to fill in the gaps). For now, however, this can suffice as an introduction to how our experiencing works. In subsequent chapters we will be discussing these processes in more detail, and how you can use them in more and less useful ways.

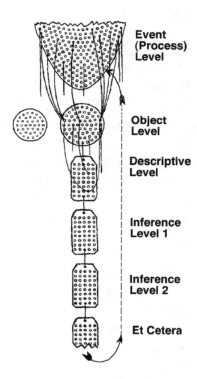

Figure 2-1 The Structural Differential

What Makes Humans Human?

Let's return to the issue of how our ability to put things into words (or any kind of symbol or representation) differentiates us from other forms of life. Korzybski pondered the question of what makes humans human and developed the notion of three classes of life: plants, animals and humans.

Plants transform energy from the sun chemically, storing it and using it to grow. Hence, in GS we call plants chemistry-binders. Animals use plant energy as food, and thus they incorporate chemistry-binding. They also transform energy into movement through space. They mark and defend their space or territory from other animals in various ways. Consequently, we call animals space-binders. Humans also use plant energy and move and therefore incorporate both chemistry-binding and space-binding. But we also have the ability to create symbols about our experiences, in the form of pictures, numbers and words. We can make signs (e.g., of unicorns and horses), write books, produce computers and computer programs, and store these products in libraries. We can create systems for distributing this information. Through the use of language, we can pass on information (and misinformation) from one person to another and from one time to another. We can evaluate our evaluations.

We do this within ourselves, as we learn from our experiences and develop our lives. We do this among ourselves as we communicate. We do this across generations so that each generation of humans has the potential to start off where previous generations ended. We utilize the experiences of the past as we develop the present and future. Accordingly, we call humans time-binders.

Using GS, we learn how to improve our TIME-BINDING capacities: how to evaluate what we inherit from the past (our own past and the pasts of others and prior generations); how to sort out misinformation and add to our store of useful information; how to most effectively create a positive present and future. Most of us are

not considered 'insane'. Yet we often have so much misinformation, we often spend so much time misevaluating situations, that
we may not act quite 'sane' either. Korzybski therefore referred
to most of us as 'un-sane'.[7] We can view general semantics as a
system for overcoming un-sanity and for living sanely.

In Susan's office, we have a picture of a unicorn on a
wall where a sliding glass door used to be. On the opposite
wall hangs a structural differential. We see these structures
as related to positive time-binding. The unicorn represents
so-called 'things' which don't exist except in symbolic form;
despite this, we may behave as if they do exist and go looking
for them. The former glass door represents things which exist
that we often don't account for (hence the mark that was in
the glass to prevent us from bumping into it, thinking it was
open when it wasn't). The structural differential represents
the general-semantics system, which helps us to avoid bumping into glass doors and shopping for pet unicorns. Using it,
we can make the most of our experiences by evaluating them
adequately, and changing our evaluations when necessary.

You may have noticed how we keep referring to "using" GS. GS in itself cannot help you. You can learn to help yourself by using GS in your daily life. As you answer the questions we ask, and experiment with what we suggest in the **Applications** section at the end of each chapter, you can begin to use GS for yourself and start to experience the benefits of working with the system. Accordingly, you can start to develop "uncommon sense".

Applications

1. What experiences have you had where you discovered you were "shopping for unicorns", i.e., expecting to find 'things' which don't exist? With what results?

2. What "glass doors", i.e., unexpected things, have you bumped into? With what results?

3. How have you repeatedly "poked yourself in the eye", i.e., failed to learn from your experiences? With what results?

4. What past learnings (your own and those you've gotten from others, including from books) have turned out incorrect or unhelpful?

5. What past learnings have turned out correct and helpful?

6. How do these questions help you to work on your personal concerns?

Chapter 3

Uncommon Sense

...I think one can live happily with questions, which are alive with promise; while however useful or beautiful answers may be, they are fossils of past questioning and discovery...When accepted as beliefs, answers shut off possibilities of new understanding, and in any case many accepted answers are just plain wrong and sometimes seriously misleading...But we do need at least tentative answers if only to make doubting and questioning effective.

Richard L. Gregory[8]

The older systems were 'common sense' perhaps of a pre-scientific era, but the new systems represent more closely 'reality' as we know it today, and uncommon *sense was and is necessary. In our work we are trying to make this modern 'uncommon sense' 'common' and workable.*

Alfred Korzybski[9]

Bruce's Aunt Marj once managed a food service for a busy government facility. One day, as she was checking the food being served in the cafeteria line, she noted that the soup container barely felt warm. She turned to one of the workers and asked him to heat up the soup. The worker stuck his unwashed finger in the soup and said that the soup was hot enough. Aunt Marj, taken aback, told him to dump the container and bring out a fresh, hot one, and directed, in no uncertain terms, that he never stick his fingers like that in the food again. Now we ask you: What might that food service worker have assumed when he stuck his finger in the soup? Do you think that the worker used 'common sense'? We would say no, by today's standards, since it's accepted among food service workers to avoid physically handling food with unwashed hands, as this can lead to the spread of bacteria and disease.

Such notions, however, have not always been accepted as 'common sense'. As late as the 1860s, it was even accepted as common practice among doctors and surgeons to operate with their bare hands, without washing them or sterilizing their instruments between patients. For suggesting that doctors should wash their hands to reduce infections, Semmelweis—one of the first physicians to criticize the common practice of the day— was laughed at by his peers and eventually dismissed from his teaching post.[10] Can you imagine what people handling food were doing? Marj's worker would feel right at home, since he was employing the 'common sense' of the 1860s and before.

Semmelweis and Pasteur, who developed the germ theory of disease (the 'far-out' notion that creatures invisible to the naked eye act as the agents of disease), practiced 'uncommon sense'. This led to what is now accepted as 'common sense' by many in the food handling, medical and other professions.

We are writing this book, in part, because we believe that human beings can no longer depend on much of present-day 'common sense' to solve our problems. How did Semmelweis, Pasteur and others come to challenge the 'common sense' notions of their time? How did their formulations come to be accepted in turn as today's 'common sense'? What 'common sense' notions do many of us take for granted that may turn out mistaken, in both our personal and collective lives?

Examining Assumptions

Korzybski pondered these sorts of questions. He had experienced at first hand the carnage of World War I on the Russian front. One of the things that struck him, besides a bullet to his knee, was the disparity between the advanced technology amassed to conduct the war (the railroads, guns, cannons, artillery, etc.)—admittedly small stuff by today's stealth bomber standards—and the social structures in collapse that had resulted in the conflict.

Sophisticated, mostly reliable, technology was used during the war and in the rest of society. It was built as the result of accumulated knowledge in science and its applications, the result of human beings learning from their experience by *becoming aware of, questioning, testing and revising their assumptions* (accepted knowledge or 'common sense'). This attitude towards assumptions (scientific method in the broad sense) appears singularly present in the fields of physical science and technology and represents the human time-binding capacity at its best.

Unfortunately, the narrow application of our time-binding capacities to such technologies as weapons research and development emphasizes the relative failure of time-binding in the social spheres. The failure to prevent World War I and the subsequent bloody course of the 20th Century—now continuing into the 21st Century—demonstrated for Korzybski a singular lack of ability to learn from our experience. The horrible imbalance between technical knowledge (such as weapons research) and social knowledge (such as human communication) has only gotten worse since Korzybski first formulated his notions. Korzybski's way out of this dilemma involved not the abandonment of science but a broadened, more generalized understanding and application of scientific method to our personal and social lives: general semantics.

None of us can live free of assumptions, premises, inferences, generalizations, etc. What assumptions are you making right now as you read this book? That your chair will continue to hold you up? That you are indeed holding a book in your hands and not in fact in bed dreaming it all up? That the sun will 'rise' tomorrow? The list could go on and on.

The fact that we are labeling these as assumptions and calling some aspect of your experience into question may seem odd. All of us take these kinds of things for granted, the authors included. Precisely these kinds of things form the basis of 'common sense', the common everyday and unreflected assumptions that we all make.

So what? Precisely those things that we assume to be so, without remaining aware that we are making these assumptions, can keep us, like the pre-Semmelweis surgeons, from finding solutions to our problems or can even create new problems. Many of our assumptions serve us well; our functioning depends on making assumptions such as expecting food in the grocery store when we go shopping. Recognizing these as *assumptions*, however, can help us prepare for the unexpected. Do you recognize that your chair may be on the verge of collapse? Can you be prepared for this possibility?

Linguistic anthropologist Benjamin Lee Whorf worked as an insurance investigator and discovered how the unconscious assumptions related to our language use could lead to accidents. Investigating the causes of fires and explosions, Whorf found that,

> ...around a storage of what are called "gasoline drums," behavior will tend to a certain type, that is, great care will be exercised; while around a storage of what are called "empty gasoline drums," it will tend to be different—careless, with little repression of smoking or of tossing cigarette stubs about. Yet the "empty" drums are perhaps the more dangerous, since they contain explosive vapor.[11]

When people start to become aware of how assumptions can lead them astray they may decide not to make assumptions. An old schoolroom slogan states, "Don't assume or you'll make an *ass* of you and *me*." However, you can't not assume. Human behavior is driven by assumptions. We can only free ourselves of the tyranny of our assumptions, of what everybody 'knows' that "ain't" so, by becoming aware of, questioning, testing and revising them when necessary.

Logical Fate

In his early writings, Korzybski emphasized the notion of LOGICAL FATE: from our assumptions, particular consequences (our conclusions, evaluations, attitudes and behavior) inevitably follow.

On the basis of fundamental assumptions, premises, etc., we build our world view ('metaphysics'). This leads to our orientation towards ourselves and others, a given situation, a problem, etc. Our assumptions and world view result in particular consequences, e.g., attitudes and behavior.

A set of assumptions can be viewed as a 'house' within which we live. Like a house that can be structurally unsound and unable to support the lives within it, our basic assumptions can lead to an inadequate world view, inadequate attitudes and behavior. How do we 'rebuild the house', find new more useful behaviors, solutions to problems, etc.? This situation is illustrated in Figure 3-1.[12]

A_1 represents our current, perhaps inadequate, assumptions or premises. C_1 represents the consequences, or conclusions, attitudes, behavior, etc., that result from A_1. A_2 represents a different, perhaps more adequate, set of assumptions, with C_2 the resulting consequences.

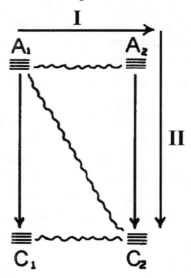

Figure 3-1 Logical Fate

The wavy lines represent the inconsistency and subsequent difficulty and frustration of trying to get to the more adequate results of C_2 without revising the old assumptions. We can get to new, more adequate conclusions, attitudes, behaviors, by first revising our old assumptions and beliefs (Arrow I) and then the new conclusions follow (Arrow II).

Korzybski derived this notion of logical fate from the work of mathematician Cassius Keyser.[13] Keyser was concerned with the relations between mathematics and human behavior. He realized that mathematics could be characterized as an extremely refined way of making our assumptions clear and of deriving conclusions from them. Keyser and Korzybski (who were friends) decided to view our everyday thinking as very poorly developed forms of mathematics. If we could bring into our everyday thinking the mathematician's concern for making assumptions or premises clear, we might be able to function more effectively.

Scientific Method

Scientists do exactly that when they are doing science— although they don't necessarily do any better than the rest of us in applying this method to their personal lives. A scientist will start with some assumption or set of assumptions, whether a vague notion or a highly developed theory. In science, as-sumptions are open to question. This questioning is done by deriving, through logic and mathematics, some consequences which can be tested through observation, and by setting up an experiment for doing so.

The observations may turn out as predicted by the theory and thus support it (notice we didn't say prove). Or the obser-vations may knock down the theory and bring it into question. Often some aspects of a theory may remain standing and some may need to be revised. Then new testable consequences are derived and new experiments and observations are made.

Thus does science grow. This process of revising assumptions is illustrated in Figure 3-2.[14]

We start with a set of assumptions labeled "A_1". Certain conclusions follow which are tested and revised as needed so that we can form a broader, more adequate set of assumptions, labeled "A_2". These in turn can be revised to form a new set of assumptions, labeled "A_3". And the process continues.

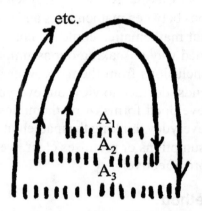

Figure 3-2 Revising Assumptions

The results of experiments may not always appear obvious. Rival theories may appear to explain what we infer is going on. Rival interpretations of experiments can be made. Yet mathematicians and scientists trust the process because it seems to have provided the most reliable way of developing useful knowledge.

Each set of assumptions leads to different consequences. The usefulness of this is not limited to formal scientific work.

In daily life revising assumptions can have a profound influence on your relationships and other aspects of your life. For example, you may assume that your relationship problems are the result of what your parents did to you. The consequences of this may include blaming them and feeling unable to solve the problems, since you can't change the past. Instead you may assume that, while your upbringing may have contributed to your relationship problems, right now you are keeping the past alive yourself by how you talk to yourself about it, etc. The consequences of this may include your changing how you talk to yourself and thus finding ways to solve your problems.

'Common sense' once told us that the earth is flat and the center of the universe. The uncommon sense of the scientific method as outlined above has demonstrated to most of us that such is not the case. What forms of today's 'common sense' need to be challenged and revised?

World Views

As the process of science has helped us to develop broader, more adequate sets of assumptions, we have come to experience some major changes in world views, or basic assumptions, about the structures of event-level happenings. New, more general, systems of explanation replaced older ones.

Major shifts occurred in mathematics and physics. The older euclidian and newtonian systems were replaced by the more modern non-euclidian and non-newtonian systems. We don't need to concern ourselves here with the details of these changes, although Korzybski studied them intensively in formulating GS.

We can note, however, that the newer systems better account for the event-level complexities we now are able to discern and infer with modern scientific equipment and formulating. For example, old notions of a separate 'space' and 'time' were replaced by Einstein's notions of a space-time continuum. We can also note that the newer systems go beyond, *and include*, the older systems, which still "work" under certain circumstances.

In later chapters, we'll be discussing GS as a non-aristotelian system which *includes*, but goes beyond, the older aristotelian system. In developing GS, Korzybski applied his knowledge of non-euclidian and non-newtonian systems. In using GS, we can get the benefits of this up-to-date knowledge in our everyday lives.

For example, our everyday evaluating can benefit through awareness of logical fate and scientific method. Have you ever wondered how your seemingly sensible neighbors could vote for *that* candidate or be in favor of *that* issue? Have you ever felt dismayed about how your friends and partners act? Don't they have any 'common sense'?

If we view their behavior in terms of logical fate, their actions may seem quite sensible given their basic assumptions, or world view, however wrong they may seem to you. We can learn to deal better with other people if we assume that they are not necessarily stupid or ogres but are operating, as are we, out of their basic unconscious and unquestioned assumptions and beliefs.

Lateral Thinking

How do we get to new assumptions, new ways of looking at the world? As we have noted, getting clear about our assumptions and their related consequences can help. So can testing them through observation and experiment, which can show us their inadequacies. However, the leap of revision itself may require something more.

The brain makes patterns. These patterns can help us to move forward. However, they can also get us stuck. Thinking skills expert Edward de Bono has classified two broad types of brain patterns which he calls "vertical thinking" and "lateral thinking". As far as we know, de Bono was not referring to "logical fate" when he formulated these. However, we can relate vertical and lateral thinking quite nicely to the logical fate diagram.

Vertical thinking, in de Bono's work, refers to logical analysis and empirical testing. It includes the elaboration and testing of patterns already present. As it happens, this relates to the vertical parts of the logical fate diagram going from A_1 to C_1 and A_2 to C_2. Although useful, vertical thinking can keep us stuck in old, familiar patterns.

By contrast, lateral thinking refers to a deliberate set of skills involved in 'shifting sideways' from one vertical pattern to another in order to revise our assumptions and point of view. Lateral thinking thus seems to correspond to the horizontal arrow going from A_1 to A_2. To promote lateral thinking, de Bono has developed a number of methods we can use consciously for jogging ourselves out of old patterns, at least temporarily, and into new, perhaps more useful ones.

Lateral thinking involves the deliberate use of provocation. For example, picking a random word and relating it to a problem under consideration can set us off on a different track. Sometimes consciously reversing one's point of view or situation can also accomplish this.

Since we often tend to become set upon a pattern rather early in our deliberations, de Bono advocates taking time to explore alternative points of view. This might involve setting a quota; for example, determining to come up with 10 alternatives. Or we might use a scheme for shifting attention from one aspect of a situation to another. For example, the PMI method involves listing the *P*lus, *M*inus and *I*nteresting aspects of whatever we're considering.

De Bono has suggested a new word, "po", suggested by *po*etry, sup*po*sition, hy*po*thesis, and *p*rovocative *o*peration, to encourage lateral thinking. We can use "po" to flag situations about which we wish to say something seemingly silly, illogical, provocative, etc. What may not seem to make sense may make sense after we have said it. Among other uses, we can use "po" as a connector for juxtaposing two disparate notions.

For example, saying "liberal po conservative" may stimulate us to see how rival viewpoints can function cooperatively within a wider political system, to note that some individuals from either grouping may not stand very far apart on some issues, etc.

These methods increase the probability of changing to more useful assumptions by getting us off our 'beaten track' of habitual perceiving and labeling. Po having a problem may not be a problem.

Applying a Scientific Attitude

Bringing our assumptions and beliefs into awareness and open to question and change can serve as a useful way to apply a SCIENTIFIC ATTITUDE in our lives. When confronted with a difficult or seemingly insoluble problem we can ask: What am I assuming about this situation? Can I assume something different? What will happen if I do? Is what I'm assuming here so? How can I test this? What observations can I make that may show that this isn't so?

Let's apply this to what you have just been reading. Some of you may feel comfortable with mathematics and science; some not. What assumptions do you make about yourself, about this material? Where on the comfort/discomfort scale do you find yourself? How much does this depend upon your assumptions?

Wendell Johnson summarized well how to apply a scientific attitude in everyday life. He developed a four-point outline:

> ...the method of science consists in (a) asking clear answerable questions in order to direct one's (b) observations, which are made in a calm and unprejudiced manner, and which are then (c) reported as accurately as possible and in such a way as to answer the questions that were asked to

begin with, after which (d) any pertinent beliefs or assumptions that were held before the observations were made are
revised in light of the observations made and the answers
obtained...after which the whole process starts over again.[15]

We can give a simple example. Children sometimes
complain that "everybody is picking on me". We can say
that they have verbalized an "observation" based on certain
assumptions about themselves and their experiences. What
clear questions might direct useful observations? We need
to clarify "everybody" and "picking on me". Perhaps, after
listing all the children in the class, the child can ask, for any
particular day, "Today, which children in my class called me
names and poked me, etc.? Which children left me alone?
Which children acted nice?" Observations are then made
and recorded. Nigh always, the child will find that perhaps a
few children are "picking", while others stay away or perhaps
even act "nice". This can lead to revised assumptions about
themselves and their experiences.

As Johnson noted, we do best by viewing this as an ongoing process, since we live in a world of ongoing change. We
do best by holding our conclusions tentatively.

Tentative Forever

For many years people believed that we could prove our
theories and beliefs if we piled up enough evidence to justify
them. However, as an old Jewish proverb states, "For example
is no proof."[16] Following the work of philosopher of science
Karl Popper, many scientists, too, have begun to question this
belief.[17] There are some theories that, because of the way they
are formulated, do not allow for any observations which could
find them incorrect, which could disprove them.

We can call these closed systems, because they can explain away any inconsistencies, etc. In the example of the child above, perhaps some children were found not to be "picking". If the child then stated, "Well, those children don't count", we could say the child had a belief system not open to disproof.

For Popper, those statements, theories, assumptions, etc., that cannot conceivably be disproved do not belong to science. For him, a scientific theory needs to take the risk that in its testing it could be disproved or falsified. From a GS viewpoint, we suggest that when dealing with serious, important issues, we do best to apply a scientific attitude and take risks in testing our statements, assumptions, etc. In this way, we can reach useful conclusions.

We want to make clear here what we are not saying, lest this sound unnecessarily serious. Using GS does not result in giving up puns, made-up words and stories, etc. We greatly look forward to this kind of activity, in fun and play, and to generate alternatives, as in lateral thinking, for further evaluation.

Philosophers are fond of using an example involving swans. A theory that "All swans are white", can be tested by observing numerous swans. If we find a black swan, our theory is disproved. If we find only white ones, have we proven our theory? Consider that a black swan could be just ahead, in the next pond. (GS scholar Dr. Stuart Mayper—a working scientist, professor of chemistry, and personal student of Popper—reported actually seeing a black swan.[18])

Thus, even those theories which we have submitted to testing and have been unable to falsify cannot be considered absolutely proven. Popper says that we can corroborate (support) a theory and that the better theories risk more because they can be submitted to more rigorous attempts to falsify them. But even these must be considered tentative forever.

As we get comfortable with this notion of "tentative forever", what Korzybski called the **"GENERAL PRINCIPLE OF UNCERTAINTY"**,[19] we can use Popper's notion of falsifiability in our everyday problem-solving. Instead of looking for ways to prove our pet theories or beliefs, we can look for evidence that might disprove them. We can look for black swans. As we suggested, a child concerned with getting "picked on" can look for children acting "nice".

If we can find no way of testing our theory in this manner, we need to consider whether we are indulging in nonsense. In the search for ways to disprove rather than justify our assumptions and beliefs, we may develop better ways to test them. We can continue to use those theories and assumptions that stand up to such testing and we can revise and retest those that do not.

What we call 'common sense', the unconscious and unquestioned assumptions that we live by, may serve us well or may get us stuck. When confronted with a seemingly insoluble problem, a first step to solution involves realizing that you are operating out of some assumptions or premises that you may not be aware of; then you may search them out so that you can test and revise them if necessary.

The process of doing this has been refined in science and mathematics. Using GS we emphasize applying this uncommon sense to our everyday lives.

Applications

1. Find someone, a friend, spouse or other family member, neighbor, writer, political figure, etc., with whom you strongly disagree about something. What assumptions do they seem to be making about the issue? (If possible, ask them.) Does what they say or do make sense when viewed in light of their assumptions? What assumptions do you make about the issue? How do they connect with your behavior?

2. The following is called the "Nine Dot Problem". How can you solve it?

> Connect all of the dots shown below, using four *connected, continuous straight* lines. In other words, do not lift your pencil from the page as you make the four lines. We suggest a pencil with an eraser.

How about connecting the dots with three lines?

> You can consult Note[20] for an explanation of how to solve this problem.

3. Consider a problem you're having. It can be a simple one. Apply a scientific attitude, by following the steps outlined by Johnson, to solve it.

4. Apply the PMI method to a problem you're having or one you've read about in the news. What results follow?

5. How do these experiments and questions help you to work on your personal concerns?

Chapter 4

Endless Complexities

For you need a sense not only of your internal landscape, but the external landscape in which it works.

Jerome Bruner[21]

We are not equipped by our orthodox educational systems...to deal with the endless complexities of the organism-as-a-whole-in-environments, which include internal *as well as external environments.*

Alfred Korzybski[22]

When Susan was a young teenager, her parents got her a much-desired electric blanket. She spent an especially warm, cozy night and happily reported this the next morning. They then discovered that the blanket was not plugged in.

Where was the warmth?

Imagine a big, juicy lemon. As I cut into it, picture the juices starting to run out. As I cut it into quarters, so I can eat it, we see just how much wonderful juice flows out. Now I start to suck on the lemon... mmmh... drinking in those juices... mmmh...

What has happened in your mouth? Tingling sensations? Watering? What caused these reactions?

Once during a family car trip, Susan's father was changing a tire and the car slipped partway off of the jack, trapping his finger. Her five-foot, two-inch tall mother lifted the car. That night her mother's back ached, she slept on the floor and the next day she felt fine. Where did her strength come from? How could she lift a car without serious injury?

Common sense suggests that five-foot, two-inch tall women can't lift cars and that lifting such a weight (or trying to) ought to cause severe injury and pain. Common sense suggests that salivation comes from food and that warmth comes from electric blankets which are plugged in. Yet in the above examples, we note that Susan's mother's strength and level of injury depended on her environment. We note that you can create "lemon reactions" without eating a lemon. Susan felt warmth not generated by the blanket.

We behave "all of a piece". We cannot divorce our sensations from our beliefs—"Electric blankets make us warm and cozy." We cannot divorce our actions from our expectations—"Lemons taste sour." We cannot divorce our reactions from our environment—"I can't act weak or feel pain now; have to save that finger." Uncommon sense involves recognizing and accepting these connections.

Evaluational (Semantic) Transactions

From a GS perspective, we acknowledge these connections. Our total behavior involves many related factors. We recognize that we don't have 'thoughts' separate from 'feelings'. We don't have 'intellect' separate from 'emotions'. We don't have a 'mind' separate from a 'body'. We don't have non-verbal separate from verbal aspects of what we do; we don't have verbal aspects separate from non-verbal ones. We don't act separately from our expectations, attitudes, beliefs, past experiences, how we talk to ourselves, how others talk to us. We formulate the model of logical fate, wherein our assumptions and behaviors are linked inextricably.

To account for these connections, we refer to human behavior in terms of EVALUATIONAL (SEMANTIC) TRANSACTIONS or simply as evaluating, defined as the organism-as-a-whole behavior of an individual in a situation in terms of the 'meanings' he or she gives to words, symbols and other events.

Although Korzybski talked in terms of "semantic reactions", we prefer talking about "evaluation" to get away from the verbal connotations that many people bring when they see the word "semantic(s)".* In his book, *The Art of Awareness*, J. Samuel Bois explicitly introduced the notion of "transaction" into general-semantics formulating. We also prefer to talk about human evaluating in terms of "transactions", which implies ongoing, circular, two-way processes between organism and environment. This gets us away from the one-directional, stimulus-response implications that the term "reaction" may at times suggest.

Our evaluational transactions can occur "internally": we remember something as funny and we laugh. They can occur "externally": someone tells a joke and we laugh. In both cases, the laugh came as a result of the 'meanings' we attached to some events. And both our "internal landscape" and our "external landscape" affect the 'meanings' we make. At times, depending on our mood, what we remembered as funny may strike us as sad. In another situation, we may decide that joking seems inappropriate and frown.

The Organism-as-a-Whole-in-Environments

In this chapter, we will discuss factors involved in our internal and external environments, or landscapes, which together influence our evaluational transactions. We will examine how you function as an ORGANISM-AS-A-WHOLE-IN-ENVIRONMENTS. We will consider how your system communicates as such an organism. We will begin to answer the question, "Where are the 'meanings'?" We like the notion of landscapes as a way of talking about our environments, in part because this allows us to emphasize the similarities and differences between humans and other organisms.

As we look out at our backyard, and work in it, we become aware of the complexities which occur as the garden grows.

---

* See "A Note On Evaluational Reactions" by GS scholar Jeffrey A. Mordkowitz in *General Semantics Bulletin* 65-68, 2001 (pp. 87-88) which thoroughly documents Korzybski's own movement in this direction.

Sun, weather and soil conditions, how the plants are ordered in relation to each other, resident rabbits and slugs, our interventions, etc., all provide an external landscape for the plants. Root and other structures which influence the ability to absorb nutrients, the individual needs of a particular plant, the effects of how the plant has been handled in the past, etc., help form what goes on inside the plant, its internal landscape.

We can create a map of our garden landscape to guide us in planning. This picture can include where the plants are placed in relation to each other, the order in which we've placed them, what structures emerge from previous owners' plantings, etc. We want our map to fit the territory of the garden as closely as possible. This can help us to avoid unwelcome surprises such as we got when we attempted to plant a tree. What were we hitting as we dug? The discovery of a buried tree stump led to a quick change in plans.

In mapping the garden, we also recognize the importance of noting subtle differences in each plant's landscape rather than assuming only similarities. We discover that the micro-climate varies considerably; within a couple of feet, we go from moderately moist soil underground to pools of water at apparently the 'same' level. Differences in light and shade created by other plantings, by the house and shed will also vary for each plant.

Similarly, we humans have complexities of internal and external influences which involve various relations, structurings and orderings. How well we map these influences, the structures we choose to consider, the evaluations we make about various orderings and relations profoundly influence what and how we do. We'll be discussing mapping extensively in later chapters.

Landscapes of 'Meaning'

As noted before, we also need to consider our differences from the plants and rabbits. In addition to such landscape factors just described, our environments include words and 'meanings'. We use language, and are surrounded by its use.

We talk about our talking. We can become aware of our assumptions and change them. We evaluate, giving 'meanings' to our experiences. Our experiences are influenced by our evaluations and those of others. We remember the past and make plans for the future. In the present, we may change our plans, based on our past experiences and expectations for the future.

We also evaluate, giving 'meanings' to, symbols other than language. When the telephone rings, our cat, Samantha, sitting near it, may startle, and then sniff around it, acting curious about the noise. We may also startle at the ring and act curious; "I wonder who that is?" As far as we know, though, Samantha doesn't evaluate in such a way that she worries, "Uh oh, I hope that isn't so-and-so. I haven't decided what I want to say to him." Or, "Oh, I hope that's so-and-so. I've been waiting for her call." Or, "Oh, no, I don't have time to talk now. Should I answer?" These complex evaluational transactions comprise an important part of our landscape.

In studying the human landscape, therefore, we need to consider 'meanings' or evaluational (semantic) factors, including linguistic factors. Such factors emerge from the complex structures of our nervous systems, especially our brains. In GS we emphasize the importance of these structures by speaking of our NEURO-EVALUATIONAL (NEURO-SEMANTIC) and NEURO-LINGUISTIC ENVIRONMENTS. (GS should not be confused with neuro-linguistic programming or NLP, although its originators, Bandler and Grinder acknowledged Korzybski in their early work.)

These neuro-evaluational and neuro-linguistic factors comprise such an important part of our landscape that we consider them at least as important a part of our environment as the sun and rain are to plants. When we speak of evaluations, we refer to our sensing-thinking-feeling-moving-doing-etc., emerging from our nervous systems and embedded in our particular neuro-evaluational, neuro-linguistic environments.

Internal Landscapes

We emphasize our nervous systems in part because they represent our connection between external and internal landscapes. What we experience comes to us through our ability to detect through the nerve endings of our eyes, ears, noses, mouths and skin. In the next chapter, we will discuss this detection process and other aspects of our nervous systems in more detail. Here we want you to start to understand the importance of your nervous system, including that fine structure, your brain, and its centrality to your organism-as-a-whole functioning.

What other internal structures are involved in your organism-as-a-whole functioning? How might such structures communicate among themselves to coordinate this functioning?

Of course, all of your internal structures or organ systems are involved in this functioning. These include your heart, lungs, stomach, liver, back, neck, joints, muscles, vocal cords, eyes, ears, nose, skin, etc. The state of any of these by themselves and in combination affect, and in turn can be affected by, your evaluations. For example, how do you attend to your environment? Do you feed your growling stomach? Do you listen to your friend? How do you transact with your environment? Does your stomach tighten up? Do you worry?

How do these states combine? Scientists have been identifying communication systems within our organisms. These systems seem to work in such a way that we can speak of psycho-neuro-physiological states. Our so-called thinking-feeling states (-psycho-) as aspects of our nervous system functioning (-neuro-) connect with the functions of our hearts, stomachs, lungs, etc. (-physiological-), resulting in our organism-as-a-whole-in-environments evaluations. 'Information' can flow so that when we hear the phone ringing, these communication systems involve our expectations, how we talk to ourselves, how much saliva we produce, our muscle tone, how and where our blood flows, etc., right down to the level of each of our cells.

Since we are presenting an introduction here, we'll only mention briefly some of the central systems involved. Information on internal communication systems has been abstracted from the work of psychologist Ernest Rossi.[23]

Let's start with the nervous system. Nerves serve as the immediate source of neurotransmitters; we can consider these as chemical messengers from one nerve cell to another and from nerve cells to other types of cells. When we form images, beliefs, words, etc., (remember the lemon? the electric blanket? the strength and pain?), neurotransmitters are produced. As they are transmitted through connecting branches, they connect with specific cells in other tissues and organs (e.g., your heart, lungs, stomach, etc.). This triggers responses in these tissue and organ cells. Thus how our nervous systems function affects not only our moods, for example, how much anxiety or depression or sense of well-being we may experience. The 'information' transmitted by neurotransmitters also affects how much warmth we feel, the production of saliva, the experience of strength and pain, etc.

Other systems also produce "messengers" which coordinate with neurotransmitters in creating organism-as-a-whole-in-environments functioning. These include the endocrine system, which produces hormones, and the immune system, which produces what Rossi calls immunotransmitters (including factors in our blood).

These messengers communicate with each other, interactively. Consequently, how we talk to ourselves and evaluate what's going on around us can influence what's happening in our stomachs, muscles, etc. Likewise, what's happening in our organ systems can influence our subsequent images, beliefs and how we talk to ourselves, in an ongoing cycle. This occurs not through some mysterious process but through the operations of our nervous systems and *neuro*-evaluational, *neuro*-linguistic mechanisms involving the psycho-neuro-physiological connections we have been talking about.

The implications of this for our health seem profound. Rossi suggests that perhaps as much as 55% of the therapeutic effect of any method of healing may result from 'placebo' responses due to suggestion, expectations and the reduction of anxiety.[24]

This may work for ill as well as good. Rossi reviews the stories reported by Walter Cannon, a highly renowned physiologist, on "voodoo" death. For example, a native was convinced that he would die after a spell had been put on him and within several days this perfectly healthy man did indeed die. Cannon speculated that his death resulted from an overloaded sympathetic nervous system due to severe emotional distress.[25]

So: Where was the warmth? What caused "lemony re-actions"? Where did the strength come from? How did the experience of pain get delayed and then felt? Where was the "spell"?

They occurred in particular organisms-as-wholes-in-en-vironments, as a function of their evaluating; the result of the total functioning of each person in an environment, from head to toe, from image to cell to image, etc.

External Landscapes

We can represent this with the following map (Figure 4-1). The arrows pointing to and from the figure represent a person's transactions with the external landscape at a given moment. Let's turn to that now.

First, we can recognize that, given the complexities of environmental influences and your influence on your environ-ments in turn, any scheme will leave out important aspects. What follows, therefore, is intended as suggestive only. Each of us has exposure to similar and different environments. None of us reacts as a stimulus-response machine to environmental influences. Rather, in our transactions each of us evaluates, differently at different times, the importance of the impact of external factors. Each of us acts on the basis of these evaluations. We encourage you to fill in gaps in our presentation where you may find them for yourself.

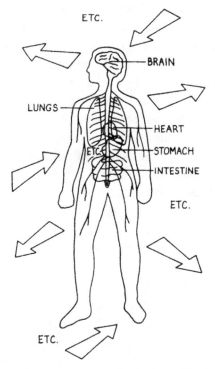

Figure 4-1 Organism-as-a-Whole-in-an-Environment

Commonly considered external factors include the weather; where we live, including such categories as rural-suburban-urban, type of house, access to leisure activities, etc.; living situation, including others in our home, how tasks are shared, how much space we have; relationships, including mate, children, other family, friends, co-workers; workplace, including type of work, work schedule, etc.; financial status; organizational affiliations and involvements, etc., etc., etc.

We can say that the impact of these factors depends in part on how they are structured, related and ordered: Do you live in a one-, two- or three-generation home? Where in the house is your room located? Do you work at home? Where in the office is your desk placed? Does your best friend work with you?

As we've noted, GS involves an interrelated set of elements. The notions of STRUCTURE, RELATIONS, ORDER represent an example of such elements. We recognize that the structure depends on the relations depend on the order depends on the structure, depends on the relations, etc. How many generations you live with, where your room is located, whether or not you work at home, etc., necessarily interconnect.

These factors impinge on us, influencing our evaluations. In turn, we influence these factors (for the most part). We can readily experience the differences that a change in the environment can influence. We often associate change in weather with a change in mood, although the direction of that change varies from person-to-person, time-to-time. Rainy days can seem cozy; sunny ones demanding of perhaps undesired activity. Sunny days can seem cheery; rainy days dreary.

We can experience the changes that occur with a new boss, an additional room in the house, a child leaving home, a new friend, etc. Susan well remembers taking the advice a co-therapist made to a couple with whom they were working: the next day she bought an inexpensive extra television set and thereby dramatically reduced family conflict.

We can consider that we each come from and live in a unique micro-culture. Even brothers and sisters grow up in different cultures, depending on their birth order, their parents' situations at the times of their births, etc. Each family develops its own culture, its set of beliefs, expectations, habits, celebrations, taboos, etc. We experience differences in neighborhood, schools, etc.

Our unique cultures include the neuro-evaluational, neuro-linguistic environments we noted above. From person-to-person, home-to-home, region-to-region we not only pronounce words and structure our sentences differently but also invest words, symbols and other events with different 'meanings'. These differences make a difference in how we function.

Each of us is born into a particular neuro-evaluational, neuro-linguistic environment that we do not choose. However, as we grow older and more responsible for ourselves, we tend to reinforce our own particular beliefs, expectations, etc., through the neuro-evaluational, neuro-linguistic environments we expose ourselves to. In the interest of growth, each of us can expose ourselves to neuro-evaluational, neuro-linguistic environments different from our habitual ones.

In line with this, philosopher Bertrand Russell wrote,

> A good way of ridding yourself of certain kinds of dogmatism is to become aware of opinions held in social circles different from your own...If you cannot travel, seek out people with whom you disagree, and read a newspaper belonging to a party that is not yours. If the people and the newspaper seem mad, perverse, and wicked, remind yourself that you seem so to them.[26]

Despite differences, we also find similarities in these environments. We often come in some degree to understand each other because we often share general word 'meanings' in common: we're likely to agree on 'objects' in a room to sit upon, although our couch may look like your sofa and not everyone regards the floor as a seat.

We also share a general language structure, which profoundly influences how we function. From a GS point of view, we consider the language structure as so important that we devote considerable space to it later in this book. We can anticipate these later discussions by pointing out some ways we've been using language here.

You may have noticed the frequent use of single QUOTES, e.g., around 'thoughts' and 'feelings' and other words that require evaluating with care. You may have noticed how we use HYPHENS to connect words that otherwise might appear to represent 'isolated' elements which, in fact, are not isolated. For example, we talk about our evaluations as involving together so-called sensing-thinking-feeling-moving-doing-etc.

Using such words as these separately without hyphens or single quotes allows us more easily to divide up our experience verbally in ways contradicted by the non-verbal 'facts'. Korzybski developed such devices as the use of single quotes and hyphens to enable us to deal with these structural difficulties. We will discuss his analysis and these and other devices in more detail later.

We want to emphasize that our evaluational transactions with our environments vary, not only among us but also within each of us over time. For each of us can only experience the environment through a unique nervous system, which not only takes in information and evaluates it uniquely but which changes ongoingly. How does the external become internal? How do we take in and evaluate such information? Read on.

Applications

1. Imagine writing your name on a piece of paper and tearing it up. Describe your evaluation of this. Now do it. How do you evaluate this? Now imagine writing your name on a piece of paper and spitting on it. Describe your evaluation of this. Now do it. How do you evaluate this? What factors are involved in your evaluations?

2. In the drawing on the next page, fill in aspects of your internal and external landscapes.

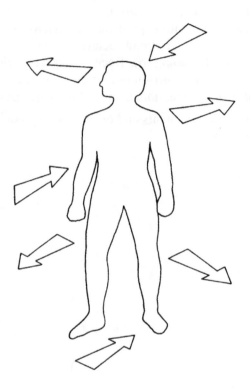

What factors do you note impacting on you? Weather? Companions or lack of them? Location? What you see, hear, smell, taste, touch? Etc. What's going on inside? What expectations, beliefs, assumptions, talking to yourself, plans, etc., do you experience? What bodily sensations and 'emotions' do you notice? Note the time and date of your evaluation, since a few moments from now your map may look different.

3. Consider your micro-culture. What rituals, values, habits, language uses, beliefs, expectations, taboos did you grow up with? (Use dates here, too, since such factors change over time.) What of these do you carry over to today? What new ones have you developed?

4. Following Russell's suggestion, pick a particular political, religious, philosophical, etc., group or outlook with which you disagree. Read the literature, publications, magazines, etc.; watch television shows, videos; attend lectures, meetings, etc., of this group (if you feel safe doing so). Become more conscious of these as neuro-evaluational, neuro-linguistic environments and of your own familiar neuro-evaluational, neuro-linguistic environments.

5. How do these experiments and questions help you to work on your personal concerns?

Chapter 5

The Process of Abstracting

We cannot make meaningful statements about some assumed..."true reality," etc. apart from ourselves and our nervous systems and other instruments....*Any meaningful scientific or existential or phenomenological statement reports on how our nervous systems or other instruments have recorded some event or events in space-time.*

Robert Anton Wilson[27]

Here I have a fan with <u>four blades</u>, when I spin it you will see a disc. But there is no disc. This is what our nervous system does... By this you see the solidity of an object where there is no object, only rotating electronic processes. We see each other as 'discs', when we are only 'rotating blades' of electricity... You must be thoroughly convinced of that process character of nature.

Alfred Korzybski[28]

As you sit reading this book, take a moment to scan your external and internal environments.

Experience the book in your hand, the hardness of the desk or chair.

Notice the shapes of the letters on this page.

What sounds do you hear?

What are you saying to yourself?

How do you 'feel' inwardly?

Read these sentences again and find out how well you can experience these non-verbally, without talking to yourself.

'Common sense' tells us that our non-verbal experiences, what we taste, touch, see, hear, smell, inwardly 'feel', etc., are the way things 'really are'. Yet when we examine the conclusions of modern sciences such as physics, neurobiology and perceptual psychology, we are led to a different view.

Our Process World

Astronomer-mathematician Arthur Eddington pointed out many years ago that the firm solid table that we see, touch and feel in the visible or "macroscopic" world consists of a buzz of activity on the atomic and sub-atomic levels.[29] The scientific 'object' is not the 'object' as you or we experience it but seems to consist of events, processes, changing relations at the level of the very small, smaller than we can view even with a microscope. We call this the "submicroscopic" level, where whirs of what we call electrons, protons, quarks, etc., and a whole 'zoo' of sub-atomic entities, relate in various ways to make the basis of what we experience as a table, a chair, an apple, you and us.

No one has ever directly seen an electron, proton or quark. These and other submicroscopic entities can only be inferred or assumed to exist. They differ from angels on the heads of pins, and other theoretical entities, because assuming their existence leads to predictable and useful results according to the scientific methods discussed previously. Various detailed predictions are made, experiments with atom-smashers, super-colliders, etc., are carried out, observations and measurements are performed and, indeed, things behave *as if* what we call electrons, etc., exist.

At the submicroscopic level of the very small, our common sense notion of 'things' doesn't hold any more. At the submicroscopic level we might more accurately talk, in the words of preeminent GS scholar Robert Pula, not of 'things' changing but of change thinging. This is illustrated in Figure 5-1.

The 'blurry' "submicroscopic apples" represent the ever-changing submicroscopic processes. The vague merging outlines indicate that the shapes and boundaries that we experience at the macroscopic level don't exist at the event level.

The "macroscopic apples" represent the 'things' or objects as we experience them. In the section below on "Our Nervous Systems", we describe how we create 'things' out of the ongoing ceaseless changing flurry of non-things.

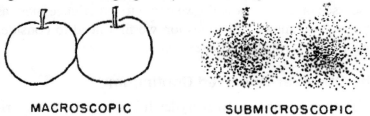

MACROSCOPIC   SUBMICROSCOPIC

Figure 5-1 Change Thinging[30]

Admittedly it requires a greater stretch of the imagination to view not only the sea wave but the water, not only the heartbeat but the beating heart, as themselves processes; slower-changing processes but processes nonetheless. Perhaps one of the main reasons that quantum physics, the branch of physics that deals with submicroscopic events, seems to defy 'common sense' involves our trying to understand it in terms of our 'common sense', macroscopic, visible world of everyday-sized 'things'.

From a GS perspective, we take as given this process view of the world. Not only at the submicroscopic level, but in our visible, macroscopic world as well, we live in a world of change 'thinging'. This view of process and change as fundamental, now supported by modern science, was perhaps first stated by the ancient Greek philosopher Heraclitus who believed that everything flows and taught that "You cannot step twice into the same river."[31]

Perhaps more clearly, as GS scholar Homer J. Moore, Jr. noted, "The river will not be the same on any two occasions that you step into it." Using GS, we seek to find ways to retain this recognition of process and change in our everyday evaluating.

How, then, do desks and chairs and other 'objects' appear
out of this submicroscopic flurry of ceaseless change, this process world depicted in physics? If desks and chairs, apples and
doorknobs, even each of us, are made up of submicroscopic
processes or events, how do we come to experience them as
'things'? To answer this question we first need to consider
each person's role as an observer.

The Observer-Observed Continuum

Both in science and in everyday life, whatever we experience, whatever we know, depends on our status as limited,
fallible observers. There exists no privileged platform, no
omniscient, 'objective' point of view for understanding the
world. Observations exist on a continuum with observers—no
observations without some observer to make them. Modern
science advanced significantly when scientists began to acknowledge the impossibility of observing and understanding
this process world without taking themselves into account as
observers.

The importance of taking the observer into account was
demonstrated by Einstein in his theory of relativity, which
established the importance of the relative motion between the
observer and the observed when measuring length or duration.
The frame of reference of the observer needs to be taken into
account, especially as speeds approach the speed of light.

Physicist Werner Heisenberg demonstrated with his
uncertainty principle the role of the observer in measuring
submicroscopic processes. It isn't possible to simultaneously
measure both the position and momentum of a sub-atomic
particle because, roughly speaking, the act of measuring one
of these affects the other.[32]

As physicist R.D. Carmichael wrote, "The universe, as
known to us, is a joint phenomenon of the observer and the
observed; and every process of discovery in natural science

or in other branches of human knowledge will acquire its best excellence when it is in accordance with this fundamental principle."[33]

In our everyday lives, as in science, we do best when we remember our own and other people's limitations as observers. To understand how, as observers, we experience 'things' in this process universe, armchair speculation will not do. We need to understand ourselves as biological organisms with nervous systems that allow us to observe and know things.

Our Nervous Systems

Whatever you experience non-verbally—an apple, an emotion, a pain, etc.—is constructed by your nervous system, your brain. You *cannot* experience the submicroscopic process apple directly; you can only experience it as it has been filtered through your nervous system. You, as an organism-as-a-whole-in-environments (internal and external) possess a nervous system that interacts with these environments both inside and outside your skin. You experience in your brain the results of these interactions. You *cannot*, we repeat, experience submicroscopic events directly. You *cannot* get outside of your nervous system to experience 'reality' as it 'really' 'is'.

In GS, the nervous system process of constructing your experience of 'objects' from the submicroscopic event level, and of representing your experience in words and other symbols, is called ABSTRACTING. The structural differential, already briefly discussed in Chapter 2, represents the ABSTRACTING PROCESS. We consider developing CONSCIOUSNESS OF ABSTRACTING in our everyday lives a basic goal of training in general semantics. In this and the following chapters we will discuss this process of abstracting in more detail, starting with a brief excursion into how your nervous system works.

You, as an organism with a nervous system, are made up of submicroscopic stuff similar to that of a desk, a tree or a wave in the ocean: electrons, protons, etc. These are organized into larger groupings such as atoms, molecules and, in the case of living things, cells and systems of cells. Animals have evolved sub-systems of cells, called nervous systems, that specialize in receiving, processing and sending information about their internal and external landscapes or environments and that allow them to move in 'space'.

Human beings possess the most elaborate nervous systems we know of, which allow us not only to move in 'space' but also to create symbols, including language. As we noted in Chapter 2, using symbols we 'bind' time. Our nervous system-created neuro-linguistic, neuro-evaluational environments allow individuals and generations to start where previous individuals and generations have left off. Standing on their shoulders, we have the potential to see further than they could and to be aware of the process. This is possible because we, as humans, possess a more complex brain than do other animals.

To act most fully human, using our time-binding capacities well, we have to allow ourselves the opportunity to more efficiently use our human brain and nervous system. GS includes methods to achieve this curbing of our immediate, automatic actions, which we call DELAYED EVALUATING. We discuss these methods in subsequent chapters.

Modern neuroscientists start from the assumption that *all* behavior depends on brain functioning, that consciousness is not separate from the workings of your brain any more than digestion is separate from the workings of your stomach, intestines, etc.[34] From a korzybskian GS perspective, we wholeheartedly embrace this. We also go a step further by insisting that what we do and say, how we evaluate and make sense of things, as products of the brain, also affect the ongoing workings of the brain. The neuro-linguistic, neuro-evaluational environments created by our nervous system evaluations can affect our brains, and thereby our other organs, just as profoundly as can the food we eat, the air we breathe and the micro-organisms we come in contact with.

Neuroscientists divide the nervous system into three parts: afferent or incoming sensory nerve fibers transmitting information from inside and outside the skin; the central nervous system consisting of the spinal cord and the brain; and the efferent or outgoing nerve fibers from the central nervous system to muscles, organs, glands and other tissues. Afferent and efferent nerve fibers, running together, make up the peripheral nervous system. These parts are represented in Figure 5-2. The system as a whole functions as a communications network among these nerve cells or neurons.

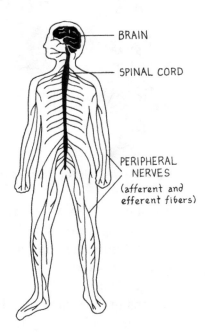

Figure 5-2 The Human Nervous System

The basic nerve cell signal, called an action potential, consists of an electro-chemical pulse traveling at speeds ranging from about 2 to 400 feet per second along the path of a neuron. Sensory nerve cell signals are triggered by particular forms of energy to which they have sensitivity, such as light, sound, pressure, chemicals, etc.

Communications between nerve cells occur at tiny junctions called synapses. An action potential will cause the release of neurotransmitter chemicals from the synaptic endings of a nerve and these chemicals will help trigger or dampen an action potential at the succeeding neuron. Similar synapses exist at the neuromuscular junction where a nerve sends impulses to a muscle to contract. Nerve cells (neurons) and synapses are represented in Figure 5-3.

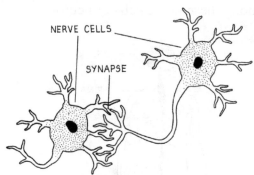

Figure 5-3 Nerve Cells and Synapses

The activities of one or even a few neurons can't account for 'thinking', 'feeling', etc. Neuroscientists are just beginning to understand how the complex interactions of large numbers of neurons operating in networks might account for the richness and variety of experience. Estimates of the number of neurons in the brain range from ten billion to one-hundred billion, interrelating by means of multiple synaptic connections.

A typical nerve cell receives input from as many as one thousand other neurons and may have as many as one thousand to ten thousand synapses. The number of possible combinations among even a small number of neurons boggles the ...well, ...brain. GS and communication scholar Kenneth G. Johnson noted that, "If the human nervous system were simple enough for us to understand it easily, we would be so simple that we couldn't."

Abstracting

Korzybski wrote that,

On the neurological level, what the nervous system does is abstracting... The standard meaning of 'abstract', 'abstracting', implies 'selecting', 'picking out', 'separating', 'summarizing', 'deducting', 'removing', 'omitting', 'disengaging', 'taking away', 'stripping', and [when used] as an adjective, not 'concrete'...The structure of the nervous system is in ordered levels and all levels go through the process of abstracting from the other levels...[35]

Let us look at the process of abstracting in neurological terms. (Refer to Figure 5-4 on page 69.)

Some happening, a space-time event inside or outside your skin, occurs at I. For example, a flash of light traveling at 186,000 miles per second occurs. Part of the energy of that event, some submicroscopic photons, represented by the first arrow, impinges on the receptor organ, your eye. Sensory neurons in the retina are stimulated.

This immediate nervous impact, labeled II, starts a chain of electro-chemical events that we have discussed already in terms of action potentials, etc. This can be considered a first-order or lower-level abstraction. The sensory neurons at II abstract information from the event at I, using the stimulating energy as a trigger for their own activity, which uses your nervous system's own store of energy. As far as we know, you do not have any experience at this level, because the impulse has not reached your brain.

Level III represents the result, at the level of your brain, of the chain of nervous system abstractings from II. At this level we have non-verbal experience: 'perceptions' (of internal and external events), 'thinking', 'feeling', etc. 'Intuitions' (generalized experience) are also included.

Level III is not Level II. Levels III and II are not Level I, the light (submicroscopic photons) traveling at approximately 186,000 *miles* per second. We do not see the light, as we have already noted, but the result of our transaction with the light, involving interacting circuits of nerve impulses traveling at an average, say, of 225 *feet* per second, a much slower speed than the speed of light.

Levels I, II and III exist on the NON-VERBAL (SILENT) LEVEL. You can demonstrate this level for yourself: Pinch a finger of one hand with the other – come on, do it! That, like our sensing of the flash of light, we call a silent-level experience. Whatever you say about the pinch is not it, because the sensation is not words!

Thus far we have been describing abstracting as it occurs in both humans and animals, where we remain on the silent or non-verbal levels. Level IV represents our uniquely human linguistic behavior abstracted from III.

Our linguistic behavior represents perhaps the most complex, electro-chemical activity known. It separates Shakespeare from Spot the dog. At this level, after experiencing the 'flash' we can do something more than bark. If in a Shakespearean mode we can ask,"But, soft! what light through yonder window breaks?"

The arrow from the verbal level to the event level indicates the important connection which we have already pointed out between the 'highest' and 'lowest' levels of abstracting. Our highest-level verbal abstractions, inferences, theories, etc., given to us by science at a particular date, provide us with our only reliable knowledge of the submicroscopic happenings, since we can never experience them directly.

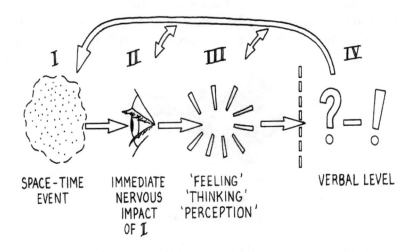

SPACE-TIME   IMMEDIATE   'FEELING'   VERBAL LEVEL
EVENT   NERVOUS   'THINKING'
              IMPACT   'PERCEPTION'
              OF **I**

Figure 5-4 The Process of Abstracting[36]

The arrows from IV to I, II and III also indicate what Robert Pula called a NEURO-LINGUISTIC FEEDBACK LOOP. They represent the circular process by which the results of our abstracting, our evaluational-linguistic behavior, influence our subsequent abstracting and other behavior, both non-verbal and verbal. We react to our reactions. Your non-verbal behavior, for example salivation, blood flow (what makes you blush?), etc., can be influenced by your linguistically-related evaluations. Remember how your mouth can water when we describe a lemon?

Perceiving

As we noted in our discussions of logical fate and feed-back loops, the basic assumptions or premises that you carry can affect how you behave and even how you perceive. Your expectations can affect what you see.

Look at Figure 5-5. What do you see? Do you see a duck or a rabbit? Can you see a duck *and* a rabbit? Can you see both at the same time? To what extent do your assumptions that this 'is' a rabbit or a duck prevent you from seeing the other figure?

Figure 5-5 Duck-Rabbit

Study of ambiguous figures like the duck-rabbit, or of 'impossible' figures like Figure 5-6, demonstrate an important point. Our perception, as a form of non-verbal abstracting, does not involve passively reflecting what our senses receive. Rather, our perception consists of our actively attempting to make sense out of cues we receive. These attempts are based on past abstracting, which includes assumptions, inferences and expectations, both verbal and non-verbal.

In a sense, we make 'bets' about what is going on. These perceptual bets, or hypotheses or inferences, are made uncon-sciously in fractions of seconds and give us some predict-ability in dealing with the incomplete information that our senses provide.

Look at Figure 5-6. There, if we start from the side with the three rounded ends, past experience leads us to bet, or guess, that they are extending out from three prongs. The figure is drawn so that from the other end we bet, or guess, that two extensions with squared edges extend from either end of a rectangular base. These two 'perceptual' bets are not compatible.

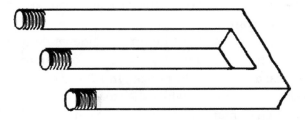

Figure 5-6 'Impossible'

Somewhere in the middle, we somehow realize that the spaces between the prongs also serve as sides of the squared off extensions. The result – a visual 'paradox' which comes from entertaining two rival hypotheses. The paradox does not exist in the drawing. It exists in us, for most of us also unconsciously assume that someone could build a 'real' figure using the drawing as a blueprint.

Our perceptual hypotheses can lead us to see things that aren't there. Seen any unicorns lately?

Bruce once went for a walk and found himself on an un-familiar street. He had a sense of dread and noticed that he was breathing faster as he looked a half block ahead under the shadow of a maple tree. A large German Shepherd dog was sitting there on his haunches. Having once been chased by one, he felt tentative about getting closer. As he did, he suddenly discovered that he was looking at a fire hydrant.

In what we perceive, as in other gambles, "you makes your bets and you takes your chances". Much of the time, but not always, in familiar situations we bet correctly. But not all situations are familiar and we can bet wrong even more often in those. The degree of shock we experience may be a function of the level of our awareness of the hypothetical, or inferential, nature of our perceptions and their dependence on our language, assumptions, etc. A higher level of awareness of this can—in the long run—help us to avoid shock, delay our immediate automatic behavior, and perhaps avoid some costly mistakes.*

Numerous accounts of hunting accidents demonstrate a similar pattern; a hunter mistakes a fellow human for a deer or other animal and shoots the person. In 1990, a hunter in Maine shot and killed a woman while she stood in her backyard. He was acquitted of manslaughter with the defense: "She looked like a deer." Greg Lemond, American bicyclist and winner of the Tour de France, was shot in the back by his brother-in-law, who mistook him for a turkey.[37]

As someone who has mistaken fire hydrants for German Shepherd dogs, Bruce can sympathize with these hunters to some degree. This represents one reason we don't trust people, ourselves included, with guns. Perhaps hunters should be required to study GS before they can get a license. People who realize the tentative nature of their perceptions and other abstractions (remain conscious of abstracting) may be less tempted to shoot first and ask questions (and have to defend themselves) later.

---

* In the short run, however, developing such awareness seems to require some shocks. Science teacher and GS scholar Thomas E. Nelson created a number of "mind-boggling, eye-rubbing," nonverbal-abstracting demonstrations, based on his work as research assistant to Adelbert Ames, Jr. and on his study of korzybskian GS. Nelson's demonstrations, and related analysis, induced students to experience the mechanisms of their own (inevitable?) mis-evaluating and nudged them to become more conscious of abstracting. See Nelson-Haber, pp. 70-73.

In this chapter, we have talked about the world as a process, how our nervous systems work, the abstracting process and the nature of 'perception'. In the next chapter, we will continue our discussion of abstracting by examining how we create and use maps.

Applications

1. To get a sense of the number of your brain cells, write out 10 billion, with all its zeros. Write out 100 billion – all those zeros!

2. Do the following, to start to get a sense of how many interactions are involved among brain cells. Write out the first 10 letters of the alphabet – a, b, c, d, e, f, g, h, i, j. Form as many combinations of these as you can. And that's only 10!

3. Look at clouds in the sky. What do you see? What else can you see? Look at a "tree" in the distance. What do you see? What else can you see? Take some time each day to play with seeing different 'things' in a familiar environment. Share these experiences with someone else, comparing 'perceptions'.

4. Do the following experiment. Fill three containers (e.g., bowls or buckets) with water: one of 'cool' water at about 40° F; another 'lukewarm' one next to it at about 65° F; another 'warm' one next to that at about 100° F. Put one hand in the container with the coolest water, while you put your other hand in the container with the warmest water. Keep them there for a moment. What do you 'feel'? Now put both hands in the center container. What do you 'feel'? What is the 'real' temperature? How do you know?

5. How do these experiments and questions help you to work on your personal concerns?

Chapter 6

Mapping Structures

"Let us remember never to forget" that all so-called knowledge or information was produced in and by some human nervous system at some time somewhere and recorded by and in those nervous systems in some sort of symbolization.

M. Kendig[38]

...we are left only with a functional, actional., [a period (when combined with another punctuation mark) stands for "etc."] language elaborated in the mathematical language of function. Under such conditions, a descriptive language of ordered happenings on the objective level takes the form of 'if so and so happens, then so and so happens', or briefly, 'if so, then so'; which is the prototype of 'logical' and mathematical processes and languages.

Alfred Korzybski[39]

Structure...what do you 'think' of when you see this word? You may picture some 'thing' like a building or its shape or form. You may distinguish this 'thing' from what it does, how it works or functions. Thus, you may distinguish "tall building" from "encloses people".

Bertrand Russell, Alfred North Whitehead and other writers noted the tendency we have to divide up the world into 'things' and what those 'things' do. They attributed this to the subject-predicate nature of English and other Indo-European languages.[40] By subjects, we refer to nouns like "building"; by predicates, we refer to what we say about the nouns, i.e. verbs like "enclose", and adjectives like "tall", etc.

Structure and Knowledge

This division between things and what they do leads to the traditional division between 'structure' and 'function', as in anatomy and physiology. In anatomy (the "subject") we might study the structure of the heart, its valves, chambers, blood vessels, etc., or at smaller levels the types of cells that make up these larger units. In physiology (the "predicate") we study what these units do; we might look at the movement of blood through the heart or the electrochemical events that occur with each heartbeat. We can say, "Hearts pump blood."

As we noted in the last chapter, the scientific study of the world has broken down the absolute nature of this division. The seemingly solid and stable structures or things of the world such as tables, chairs, buildings, hearts and brains, etc., can be viewed at the submicroscopic level as happenings, doings or functions—as change thinging.

In this view, we can verbally split say, your heart from your heartbeats; however, *both* terms refer to processes, activities, etc., that aren't in fact separable in the non-verbal world.

In general semantics, therefore, we use the word structure in a much broader sense. For example, we may talk about the structure of your heart and the structure of your heartbeat; the structure of the non-verbal world and of various processes within it; the structure of your nervous system; the structure of your experiences, perceptions, behavior, etc.; the structure of language, etc.

Structure as a basic term in korzybskian GS refers to a complex or pattern of relations. Some relations are called symmetrical. For example, the relation of 'spouse' can be considered symmetrical; if Susan is the spouse of Bruce, then Bruce is the spouse of Susan.

However, many relations can be considered asymmetrical. 'Husband' and 'wife' represent asymmetrical relations.

If Susan is the wife of Bruce, it does not follow that Bruce is the wife of Susan. We cannot reverse the order and make sense. Similarly, we cannot reverse the dates of events; as of this date, we can't unboil an egg, we can't go backward in time to undo something.

Therefore, ultimately most relations involve asymmetrical order: before and after; younger, older; first, second, third, etc.; bigger, smaller; more, less; etc.

Science and mathematics involve a search for structure in this expanded sense of relations and order. Indeed, Korzybski viewed STRUCTURE AS THE ONLY CONTENT OF KNOWLEDGE. To explain what he intended by this we need to talk about maps.

Mapping

The structure of maps and the MAPPING PROCESS gives us a way of talking about the structure of the world and of how we make sense of and talk about it. In other words, it provides a useful way of talking about how we gain knowledge through the process of abstracting.

Stephen S. Hall has written about how the notion of maps and mapping has expanded since the early 20th Century. He noted the entry for "map" in the 1910 *Encyclopedia Britannica* which defines a map as "a representation, on a plane and a reduced scale, of part or the whole of the earth's surface".

Hall pointed out, "That narrow, land-based definition has been conceptually overwhelmed since the end of the Second World War. A whirlwind tour of the world captured by modern mapping extends from the atomic to the cosmic."[41] Astronomers have mapped the surfaces of the moon, Mars and Jupiter. Biologists have mapped chromosomes, genes and DNA. Neuroscientists have mapped areas of the brain involved with vision, touch, remembering, etc.

Indeed the notion of mapping has expanded to include any form of visual representation of information. Thus did mathematicians David and Gregory Chudnovsky map the first million digits of pi, an indefinitely expanding number that results from dividing the circumference of a circle by its diameter. Pi has intrigued mathematicians for centuries and the Chudnovskys hoped to discern some patterns from their visual picture of pi that they might not see by just analyzing equations. Their map of pi, *Pi-Scape, 1989* might well hang in an art museum.[42]

Korzybski expanded the notion of mapping further. He found the mapping process a useful analogy for any form of representation. These forms include perceptions, pictures, movies, videos, equations, words, etc. He viewed the abstracting process as a representational or mapping process.

What do we do when we make a map or representation of some territory? The territory has some sort of structure; on an approximately north-south axis, Philadelphia lies between New York and Baltimore. A useful map or representation of this territory must have some similarity of structure to the territory. Therefore, our map will show Philadelphia between New York and Baltimore and not Baltimore between New York and Philadelphia.

An accurate map gives us some predictability in dealing with the territory it represents. We want to be able to predict what city we'll reach at what point by following our map. If our maps inaccurately lead us to expect to reach Baltimore about noon when we're driving from New York, we may experience disappointment and a need to change our plans when we actually end up in Philadelphia for lunch.

When the relations our maps show do not fit, that is, do not appear similar in structure to the territories we seek to represent with them, these maps may lead us astray. When we discover this, we do best to revise them. We can readily note the futility of insisting that Baltimore and Philadelphia change places to suit our maps and thus our expectations. In other areas of our lives we may less readily give up trying to fit territories to our maps.

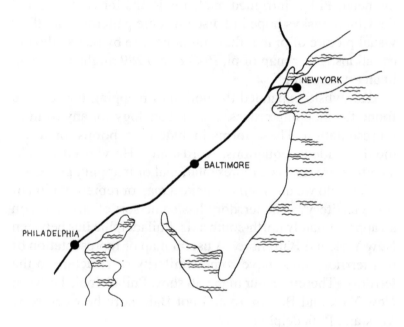

No matter how much similarity of structure exists between a map and some territory, as Korzybski pointed out, the MAP IS NOT THE TERRITORY. We call this the premise of NON-IDENTITY. A representation, a map, picture, description, etc., is not identical with what it represents, its territory. If map and territory were equivalent in all respects, in other words, identical, then what use would the map serve? Imagine trying to navigate from Philadelphia to New York with a map of New Jersey identical to New Jersey. How well would it fit inside your glove compartment?

Since a map is not the territory, then it also doesn't cover all of the territory. The relations shown on the map may have some similarity of structure to relations within a given territory. However, it necessarily must leave out many relations, structures, etc., that exist within the territory. Depending on our purposes we may leave out different relations and include others. That's part of what makes our maps useful to us. We call this the premise of NON-ALLNESS. Maps cannot include all of what they represent.

Imagine that you were trying to make a map that included everything in the room that you are in now. An impossible goal, given what we have said so far. However, let's explore the task a bit further. Let's say you've attempted such a map or picture. You've included everything in the room you could think of. Have you included yourself making the map? Okay, so now you revise your map and include a representation of yourself making the map. Hold on! Now you have made a map of yourself making a map. However, to make a 'complete' map you now have to revise this second map to include your making a map of yourself making a map and so a third map must be made and on and on and on. This could go on indefinitely.

We call this the premise of SELF-REFLEXIVENESS. Among the structures that we can make maps about, we have the previous maps we have made. We can make maps of our maps, etc. We can use language to talk about language.

Functional Functioning

We live, then, in a process world of difference and change; a world of structure, made up of a complex of relations and multidimensional order. Korzybski liked to quote Keyser, "To be is to be related."[43]

To gain knowledge of this world, we seek to create structures, our maps of the world, similar in structure to the structures of the world we are mapping. A scientific attitude, found in what Korzybski referred to as "physico-mathematical methods", consists in large part of ways of using language and seems well-suited to mapping this world of relations.

Even if mention of "physico-mathematical methods" puts you off, please stick with us for this brief discussion. It provides important background for what follows, as we learn how to make our language express, as well as possible, relations found in the process world of differences and change. Without becoming scientists or mathematicians, we can learn some mathematical ways of using language to improve our everyday evaluating.

We will focus first on the notion of FUNCTION, using it in a different sense than "what something does". In the mathematical sense, function refers to how 'things' are related. An example can be found on page 72: "The degree of shock we experience may be a function of the level of our awareness..." This statement expresses a relation between "degree of shock" and "level of awareness"; as level of awareness goes up, degree of shock goes down.

In the above paragraph, we put 'things' in quotes. We can now get more mathematical in our discussion of 'things' by introducing the term VARIABLES. We can recognize that, as stated, we don't know how much shock we're talking about when we say, "degree of shock"; we don't know the extent of awareness in "level of awareness". Other examples of variables include back pain, anxiety, excitement and fatigue. Because each of these terms can be assigned different values, from lower to higher, depending on circumstances, we refer to them as variables.

Thus, a variable consists of any indeterminate entity that can be assigned a range of values. Variables take on specific values, particular degrees and levels, as we get specific in describing the how-where-when of structural relations and order.

Scientific descriptions indicate how variables are dependent on each other; how they change in relation to each other. In mathematics, these dependencies, or functions, are symbolized as y=f(x).

This is stated as "y equals f of x", or "y is a function of x". Here "y" and "x" stand for variables and "f" stands for a functional relation between them. In this equation, "y" is called the dependent variable; "x" is called the independent variable; the value of "y" is dependent on the value of "x".

Thus, as an example, we can say that the "quality of our human relationships" (y) equals (=) a function (f) of "understanding assumptions and their consequences" (x). "Quality of relationships" is viewed as dependent on "understanding assumptions and their consequences".

This can be charted in the form of a graph which expresses the relations. Look at Figure 6-1. Here we chart a hypothetical relation between "quality of relationships" and "understanding assumptions and their consequences". Please be aware that if we were doing a formal scientific study, we would have to do much more to define and describe our variables and to make measurements of some kind.

Since our primary purpose here involves encouraging you to begin speaking in terms of functions, variables, etc., we can make do without numbers. Instead, we show the relations involved. As Korzybski said, "Structurally, when we use the language of functions, variables., [etc.] we automatically introduce extensional [factually-oriented] structure..."[44]

On the horizontal line, called the "x" axis, we place "Understanding Assumptions-Consequences". On the vertical line, called the "y" axis, we place "Quality of Relationships". For each value of "x", marked along the horizontal line, we can find the corresponding value of "y" along the vertical line. We can then mark off the points on the graph where the two values intersect. We thus show how when one changes, the other also changes. As "understanding assumptions-consequences" increases, "quality of relationships" increases.

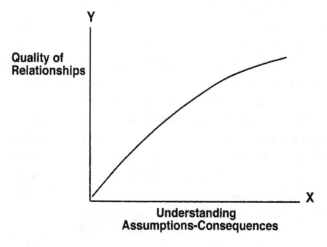

Figure 6-1 A Functional Curve

Wendell Johnson called the functional curve, "The symbol of science," regarding it as "a universal symbol of science and of the scientific way of life...It represents what any scientist strives to express: a variation of one kind, a variation of another kind, and the relationship between them."[45]

The functional relations expressed by such a curve also help us to predict more accurately. When we can describe (assign a value to) one factor, we can determine the values of factors to which it is functionally related.

You can begin to search for functions and variables in situations that you deal with every day. Some of the functions that we notice in our work with people include the following. People's back pain may be a function of their posture-movement habits, the types of chairs they sit in, the particular states of their muscles and joints, their levels of anxiety, etc.

People's 'emotional' states may be a function of how they talk to themselves, the types of interpersonal relationships they have, their goals for the future, their family history, how much caffeine they consume, etc.

Notice that a particular 'effect', such as back pain or 'emotional' distress, will probably be a function of multiple variables, commonly called 'causes'. A particular 'effect' can serve also as a 'cause'. For example, back pain can function as a cause of 'emotional' distress.

Conversely, a particular 'cause' will probably serve as a variable in a number of different functions with multiple effects. For example, what you say may have a number of interpretations depending on the listeners, their expectations, etc. What you do may have a number of different effects beyond your intended consequences. In dealing with any complex system or set of relations, it seems useful to remember what biologist Garrett Hardin called the first law of ecology, "You can never merely do one thing."[46]

Any functional relation we note constitutes a map we've created. Therefore, it also seems useful and necessary to remember that it is not the territory. It needs to be examined, tested and rejected or modified as needed.

Non-Additivity

Some relations occur relatively simply and directly. For example, suppose you have invited a close friend over for dessert and four more people unexpectedly arrive at your door. In resetting the table, you can add one plate and one mug for each new person. Thus, we can say that for each new person (independent variable) you add two new pieces of china (dependent variable). This relation is called additive.

Additive relations can be exemplified by the function $y=f(2x)$. The value of y grows additively, by 2, as x increases by 1. So we have 2, 4, 6, 8, 10, etc. Each succeeding value of y results from *adding* a fixed amount (in this case 2) to the preceding value. This relation also is called linear because its curve is drawn on a graph as a straight line (Figure 6-2).

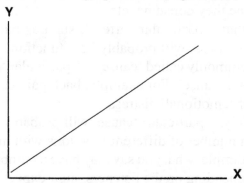

Figure 6-2 An Additive, Linear Function

We can contrast this with non-additive relations, which can be exemplified by the function $y=f(2^x)$. The value of y grows non-additively; so we have 2, 4, 8, 16, 32, etc. Each succeeding value of y results from *multiplying* by a fixed number (in this case 2) the preceding value of y. This relation is called non-linear because its curve is drawn on a graph with a changing slope, not a straight line (Figure 6-3).

Modern mathematics, including the misleadingly named 'chaos' theory,[47] helps us to clarify, express and graph, and thus better understand, non-additive relations. It provides us with a language well-suited to talking about what we refer to as multidimensional order, the complex causes and effects, relationships and changes in the process world as we now understand it.

Most of our most important relations involve such complex factors. A simple example involves the start of a family. 2 (parents) + 1 (baby) = much more than a simple 3; an entirely new complex of relations develops.

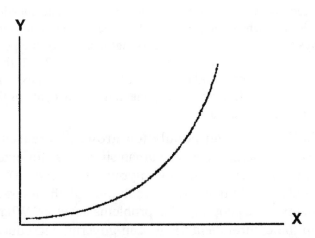

Figure 6-3 A Non-Additive, Non-Linear Function

Let's return to our dessert party. What happens to human relationships as four more people arrive? Perhaps you had intended an intimate one-to-one talk with your friend. Your expectations may not as easily be reset as the table. We do not have a simple 2+4=6 situation. What occurs as each new person gets added?

For each additional person, the number of relationships increases non-additively. You can close your eyes and imagine you and your close friend starting to talk; the door bell rings; now open the front door and admit four more people; they all greet each other, you greet each one; as you get out the additional mugs and plates, you adjust your expectations and consider how you all will get along...

Ecologists Paul and Anne Ehrlich gave the following example of non-additivity:

A key feature of exponential [non-additive] growth is that it often seems to start slowly and finish fast. A classic example used to illustrate this is the pond weed that doubles each day the amount of pond surface covered and is projected to cover the entire pond in thirty days. The question is, how much of the pond will be covered in twenty-nine days? The answer, of course, is that just half of the pond will be covered in twenty-nine days. The weed will then double once more and cover the entire pond the next day. As this example indicates, exponential growth contains the potential for big surprises.[48]

Similarly, human population growth increases non-additively, as do many other human situations (for example, compound interest on money in your bank account). What increased non-additive effects result through the interactions of so many more people? What problems develop? What happens to the environment? How can government, education, etc., best function given these complexities?

It seems that many of our political leaders still consider these, as well as other situations involving non-additive factors, in an additive way. This may have a great deal to do with what Korzybski referred to as our "collapsible" social structures. We and they might do better to look for non-additive functions as we seek to make uncommon sense of things, avoid unwelcome surprises, and develop stronger social structures.

Consciousness of Mapping

To review what we have said so far, we live in a process world, a world of structure, a complex of relations involving multidimensional order. Knowledge involves having representations, or maps, that have some structural similarity to whatever situations, things, etc., we represent. We use the analogy of maps to talk about this. Maps have three important characteristics that serve as basic GS premises or assumptions:

1. **A MAP *IS NOT* THE TERRITORY.** (For example, words *are not* the things they represent.)

2. **A** MAP COVERS *NOT ALL* THE TERRITORY. (For example, words cannot cover all they represent.)

3. **A** MAP IS *SELF-REFLEXIVE*. (For example, in language we can speak *about* language.)[49]

We function better when we build our maps by evaluating in terms of structure, relations, order and function. Looking for multiple variables in situations, looking for non-additive factors, will help reduce the number of unpleasant surprises in our lives because we will begin to expect the unexpected.

We humans orient ourselves by means of our models or maps, which include assumptions, premises, etc. To the extent that we remember this and the preceding general-semantics premises, we will question our maps and, as scientists do, revise them when necessary. In these ways our evaluational transactions will appear more sensible (sense-able?) and we'll less likely find ourselves on major expeditions hunting unicorns.

Such sense-able behavior seems more likely when we are conscious of abstracting. In the next chapter, we will review the structural differential and discuss it in more detail, especially in relation to the process of mapping.

Applications

1. Listen to something (music, the sounds you hear outdoors, a group of people talking, etc.). What "structures" emerge as a function of your hearing? What relations and order can you discern? Draw a picture of those sounds.

2. What do you know about your home? How do you know this? What role do "structures", "relations", "order" play? What 'is' your home 'really' like? How do you know?

3. Make a picture of one room in your house, while in a different room. Then go into the room you're mapping and add, in a different

color, things and details you left out. What else can you add? What else? Stop when you have it 'all' (or before you faint from hunger).

4. Write down five functional relations that you are aware of. Express them in the form "y is a function of x, etc." For example, how tired I feel (dependent variable) is a function of how many hours I've been up, etc., (independent variables). List as many independent variables as you can for each functional relation.

5. Choose a particular factor or variable, for example, reading this book. How many other factors are functionally related to it (what 'causes' this 'effect')?

6. Choose a particular factor or variable, for example something you intend to do. How many other factors may be affected by it (what 'effects' may it 'cause')? What unintended consequences may result?

7. Begin to notice non-additive effects. When does a seemingly small change have a large, perhaps unexpected, effect?

8. How do these experiments and questions help you to work on your personal concerns?

Chapter 7

The Structural Differential

So it is that the brain investigates the brain, theorizing about what brains do when they theorize, finding out what brains do when they find out, and being changed forever by the knowledge.

Patricia Smith Churchland[50]

As a rule, unless they are very unhappy, people try to trust their 'understanding', and dislike to train repeatedly with the Differential. For some reason or other, they usually forget that they cannot acquire structural familiarity with, or reflex-reactions in, spelling, or typewriting, or driving a car, [etc.] by verbal means alone. *Similar considerations apply in this case. Without the actual training with the Differential, certainly the best results cannot be expected.*

Alfred Korzybski[51]

Korzybski developed the structural differential as a teaching device to help people become more conscious of abstracting in their daily lives. It fleshes out Figure 5-4, in Chapter 5, on the process of abstracting. In some ways it might be considered a summary of the general-semantics system.

Korzybski used the structural differential throughout his teaching and writing. This use included building three-dimensional models of it. He considered it important for his students to handle the model and to point to the diagram while explaining it to themselves and others. He also encouraged his students to use the diagram to help themselves evaluate specific life issues and problems. Like much of GS, it may appear deceptively simple on a verbal, 'intellectual' level. We heartily suggest that you use it as a tool for evaluating and problem-solving. We refer to our own charts frequently. See the next page for the structural differential diagram (Figure 7-1).[52]

Levels of Abstracting

The structural differential represents different levels and processes (structures) involved in abstracting. By keeping it in front of you as you evaluate and formulate, you can differentiate and avoid identifying these different structures, which exist on different levels or orders of abstraction.

A parabola with broken-off edges on top represents structure$_1$—the submicroscopic event (process) level. This corresponds to Level I in the Process of Abstracting diagram (Figure 5-4, p. 69)—some space-time happening inside, outside or on the skin.[*] The small circles or holes within it represent individual details, characteristics or aspects we ascribe to such an event; what we infer is going on. The broken-off edges indicate that the parabola extends indefinitely. We can never exhaust the details, which go on and on, etc.

The large circle below the parabola represents structure$_2$ —what we call the object level, the level at which we experience so-called 'objects' of perception including 'things' we see, touch, taste, smell, etc., as well as toothaches, feelings, non-verbal contemplating, etc. The strings hanging down from the parabola dangle freely or connect to holes in this circle and represent the process of abstracting. That is, certain characteristics from the event level are left out and others are included or selected by our nervous systems. Our perceptions consist of this nervous system mapping of an event.

---

* Tom Nelson suggested revising the parabola (which includes each of us, and what's inside and on our skin) to explicitly "include the nervous system. It can be done quite simply with the structure from mathematics called the Mobius-strip, where the one-sided object becomes the nervous system intermeshing with some event." See Nelson, p. 75.

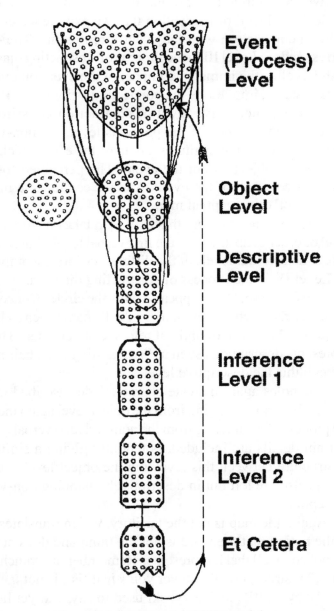

**Event
(Process)
Level**

**Object
Level**

**Descriptive
Level**

**Inference
Level 1**

**Inference
Level 2**

Et Cetera

Figure 7-1 The Structural Differential

We use a circle to represent this level to indicate that a particular 'object' of perception that we experience appears finite in comparison with the event it represents. The circle corresponds to Level III in the Process of Abstracting diagram, with Level II, the immediate impact of the event on our nervous systems, implied by the connecting strings.

As each successive level of abstraction constitutes a representation or map of the previous level, the non-verbal perceptual 'object' constitutes a map of the event level. The perceptual 'object' is not the event. The perceived 'object' does not cover all of the event. And we can make a map of this 'object' or perceptual map.

Once we start talking, this new map takes us to the next level or order of abstraction, the first verbal level. This, and the subsequent verbal levels of the differential, are encompassed by Level IV in the Process of Abstracting diagram.

The first verbal level appears below the circle. Concerning single terms, it represents an individual's name such as Bruce or Susan. More importantly, it refers to statements. Thus, it represents descriptions such as "I am sitting in a chair now." We call this the descriptive level.

The holes again indicate characteristics ascribed to this level. The strings hanging from the object level again indicate the process of abstracting from the non-verbal to verbal orders. Certain details are included, potentially giving a similarity of structure between this level and the object level. Certain details also are left out in descriptively mapping non-verbal perceptions.

Again, the map is not the territory, which translates here as the notion that the word is not the thing and does not and cannot cover all that it represents. Remember the "pinch your finger" instruction? Whatever you *say* it 'is', is not *it*.

"Baby stuff!", as Korzybski used to say, and yet human beings constantly act *as if* the map 'is' the territory, as if the word 'is' the thing. Much of advertising seems to focus on getting us to respond to words and images as if they were identical to the particular product being sold.

The column "Selling It" in *Consumer Reports* provides good examples of this. In one, they show the front label from "Snak Club Old Fashion Red Licorice." They write, "We were charmed by its slogan, 'A meal in itself.' Who needs the basic food groups when you can dine on corn syrup, wheat flour, citric acid, and artificial flavor and color?"[53] About a men's store which advertised a sale featuring "A Complete Wardrobe For Men Under $100," they write that the "complete wardrobe consisted of a blazer, shirt, tie, and belt. But, as the reader who sent us the clipping asked, shouldn't a gentleman's wardrobe include trousers? The belt would look funny without them."[54] Were we to follow the suggestions of these ads and act as if the word 'is' the thing, we'd end up malnourished, cold, and possibly arrested.

The second hanging label represents a second-order verbal abstraction or mapping of the first-order description. The numerous strings have been omitted to streamline the diagram; however the process of abstracting continues. At this level, a statement about a statement, we go beyond description of the non-verbal experience. This and subsequent levels of statements about statements about statements, etc., indicated by the two labels underneath it, include inferences, assumptions, premises, conclusions, hypotheses, generalizations, theories, etc. We call these the inference$_1$ and inference$_2$ levels.

The self-reflexiveness of this mapping process, the notion that we can continue to make statements about our statements and generalizations about our generalizations, is indicated by the broken-off label at the bottom of the diagram. The broken edges symbolize that this process can go on indefinitely. We indicate this by noting "et cetera". We can take this label to represent the highest-level inferences we can make at a given date.

The arrow from the broken-off label to the broken-off parabola represents, as previously noted, that whatever we know about the non-verbal event level, the parabola, we know only from such verbal higher-order inferences and theories. Our scientific knowledge at a given date, inferential in character, gives us the most reliable knowledge of the process level, more reliable than our 'naked eye' sense data. Korzybski referred to this as "the circularity of human knowledge".[55]

The connecting arrow also represents a segment of a neuro-linguistic feedback loop. In a spiral fashion, our verbal behaviors affect our subsequent abstractions and behavior and form part of the world that we (and others) transact with. Be careful what you say to yourself. You may be listening.

Korzybski originally developed the structural differential to show the difference between human beings and other animals. The smaller circle with no strings attached to either the parabola or to the labels represents the animal 'object'. With the lack of strings, we don't intend to suggest that an animal, say a dog or cat, doesn't abstract. No strings indicates that animals don't appear to have the potential for consciousness of abstracting.

Animals may show some symbolic or pre-symbolic behavior. However, because animals lack sufficiently complex nervous systems, they cannot, as far as we know, talk—and talk about their talking. Their abstracting stops at a certain limited point. Even though chimps can use tokens or gestures as 'symbols', they have not invented chimp science, as far as we know, and therefore do not know or have the potential to know that they abstract. Insofar as we humans don't behave with consciousness of abstracting we copy other animals in our nervous systems and fail to live up to our human potential.

Identification

This copying of animals involves what we call IDENTIFI-
CATION. Identification involves confusing levels or orders of
abstraction by assuming that two structures existing at different levels are exactly the 'same' in all respects. So a hunter
doesn't question but assumes that his perception of a deer is
the same as an actual deer and thus shoots a woman in her
backyard. A study was done on someone with hay fever who
developed allergy symptoms when exposed to roses—paper
ones.[56] In these examples, people identify their non-verbal
abstractions, their perceptual objects, with the events.

Perhaps it is not possible for human nervous systems not
to identify in this way to some extent on the non-verbal level.
However, the awareness that our 'perceptions' constitute abstractions and are not 'it' can add some degree of delay and
flexibility to our behavior. We can increase our chances of
checking further before we shoot or sneeze.

The hunter, using the structural differential, might avoid
saying, "That is a deer," instead saying, "That looks like a
deer to me. Let me check further before I shoot." The allergic
person might examine the paper roses, check out the non-
verbal territory and find out to what extent behavior changes
when this is done.

Confusing verbal with non-verbal levels appears common.
As we mentioned, much of advertising operates by promoting the identification of verbal with non-verbal levels. Alan
Watts commented on some people's tendencies to eat the menu
instead of the meal when they go to a restaurant.[57] Have you
ever felt disappointed because what you ordered wasn't what
the words on the menu 'meant' to you?

The first time Susan ordered chicken cacciatore in a
restaurant, she 'suffered' a little shock. Her "menu" for this
dish, as she grew up with it, was chicken cooked in a tomato

sauce, to which Velveeta cheese had been added, served over
elbow macaroni. Delicious, but not quite an Italian version
(also delicious, she learned).

Speech professor and GS scholar Irving J. Lee told the story
of going to a dinner party where a wide variety of delicious food
was served buffet style.[58] After people were well into enjoying
the food and conversation, the host pointed to a silver platter
containing some meat and asked his assembled guests, "What do
you suppose that stuff was?" The guests guessed pork, chicken,
etc. The host said, "Snake steaks!" One young woman appeared
especially affected by this announcement, turned pale and, as Lee
delicately put it, saw her dinner for the second time.

Up to the point that the host made his announcement, no
one had any negative evaluation. Sticks and stones can break
your bones and words can make you queasy or crazy, the more
so when you identify them with what they symbolize.

"Businessmen are greedy." "Boys will be boys." "If you've
seen one, you've seen them all." Insofar as we react to different and changing individuals in terms of our categories, as if
they were 'the same as' our categories, we identify. Insofar as
we do this, we misevaluate, unfairly prejudging any particular
individual with whom we are dealing. In other words, we fail
to remain conscious of abstracting, of our role in categorizing.
Our decisions become static and inflexible. We can't avoid using
language to classify and categorize, but we can use language
with awareness that we are doing it. In later chapters, we'll be
examining issues of categorizing in more detail.

Identifying levels of abstraction also occurs when people
confuse their inferences, generalizations, etc., (higher-order
verbal abstractions) with descriptions (lower-order verbal
abstractions). Any so-called statement of 'fact' contains some
assumptions. However, we can still have relatively 'neutral'
descriptions or reports such as "I see a light in the sky." These
statements can point someone else to something observable.

Another declarative statement such as "I see an extraterrestrial spacecraft" appears similar to the first, yet it involves going way beyond what can be directly observed. This creates a problem, if we aren't aware that we are doing this.

Problems at this level also involve formulating a higher-order abstraction, like 'mind', and assuming that some 'thing' must therefore exist in the non-verbal world that exactly corresponds to it. This brings us back to the subject-predicate structure of our language. Neurologist Peter W. Nathan—not knowledgable about GS as far as we know—writes in, ironically enough, *The Oxford Companion to the Mind,*

> For the neurologist, there is no such thing as the mind. There are certain activities of the brain endowed with consciousness that it is convenient to consider as mental activities. Since one expects to find a noun adjoined to an adjective, one supposes that there must be a mind expressing itself in a mental way. But the requirements of language and of logical thought are not always the same; demands of syntax may lead to errors in thinking."[59]

Indeed, the search for our own and other people's identifications can provide limitless entertainment, enlightenment and practice.

The process of abstracting results, then, in non-verbal object-level abstractions—traditionally called 'perceptions', and linguistic or verbal abstractions (formulations) such as descriptions, inferences, generalizations, etc.—traditionally known as 'concepts'.** These products of the abstracting process map, or represent, preceding levels or orders. Their only 'truth' comes from similarity of structure with what they represent, which ultimately comes down to the predictability they give us to deal with ongoing non-verbal events.

** Various kinds of signs and symbols occupy an interesting, fuzzy middle ground between non-verbal 'perceptions' and verbal 'concepts'. As Tom Nelson noted, we *could* specify "many, many object levels, internal as well as external." See Nelson, p. 75.

'Natural' (Appropriate) Order of Abstracting

Personal and interpersonal problems result when we identify. Identifying different orders of abstraction, we assume and act as if our non-verbal and verbal maps are the same as what they represent, as if the map is the territory. For example, we may act as if people 'are' what we call them—"stupid", "lazy", etc. We may eat the menu instead of the meal and orient ourselves according to verbal definitions instead of 'facts'. We call this INTENSIONAL behavior. Note that we spell this word with an "s". Don't confuse this with the word "intentional".

When we behave intensionally, our maps become more important than what we are mapping. Our inferences become more important than descriptions, our descriptions more important than non-verbal experience. We may say, or imply by our behavior, "My 'mind' is made up. Don't confuse me with 'facts'." And we treat our non-verbal experiences or 'perceptions' as if they do not differ from the non-verbal world.

In other words, we reverse what Korzybski called the 'NATURAL' ORDER OF ABSTRACTING; 'natural', if we remain conscious of abstracting. (Since reversing the order seems only too natural for most of us, perhaps—as Stuart Mayper suggested—we should say the "appropriate order of abstracting.") To evaluate more appropriately, we orient ourselves to events first, then our 'perceptions', then descriptions, inferences, etc. The non-verbal levels are given primary importance. The verbal levels have secondary importance and ultimately ought to direct us back towards lower-order, non-verbal abstractions, toward silent-level observation.

When we give priority to 'facts' or non-verbal happenings rather than verbal definitions and labels, and maintain our consciousness of abstracting, we call this EXTENSIONAL behavior. We will discuss INTENSIONAL and EXTENSIONAL ORIENTATIONS in more detail later. We will show you practical techniques called the EXTENSIONAL DEVICES for speaking, writing and acting extensionally—ways of using language instead of getting 'used' by it. Using the structural differential will also help you to do this.

Applications

1. Using the structural differential, explain the process of abstracting to someone else.

2. The next time you experience disappointment, ask yourself what higher-order abstractions of yours were violated by your experience of the moment. What will happen to such disappointments when you hold your higher-order abstractions more tentatively?

3. Become aware of any tendencies you may have to act as if you're saying, "My 'mind' is made up. Don't confuse me with 'facts'." What might you risk in "unmaking" your generalizations and considering new information? What might you gain?

4. Using the structural differential, evaluate a problem you are having. As you describe the problem to yourself, note which aspects of it involve non-verbal experiences/behaviors. Which aspects involve descriptions, inferences, generalizations, etc.? Note how you talk to yourself about your problem, and what effect that self-talk has on you. *Point* to each level as you do this evaluation. What do you learn about your problem and possible solutions as you do this?

5. How do these experiments and questions help you to work on your personal concerns?

Chapter 8

Non-Verbal Awareness

...one can discover through sensing, how hindering tendencies come about. As the individual becomes more sensitized and learns to befriend himself [herself] with the potentials he [she] gradually uncovers, the way slowly opens to a fuller experiencing and deeper relating to himself [herself] and all activities of daily living.

Charlotte Selver[60]

Our actual lives are lived entirely on the [object] levels...the verbal levels being only auxiliary, and effective only if they are translated back into first order un-speakable effects...all on the silent and un-speakable [object] levels...where the retraining of our s.r. [semantic (evaluational) reactions] has had beneficial effects, the results were obtained when this 'silence on the [object] levels' has been attained, which affects all of our psycho-logical reactions and regulates them to the benefit of the organism and of his [her] survival adaptation.

Alfred Korzybski[61]

Four Zen students made a vow to remain silent for seven days. On the first day they all meditated silently as planned. No one spoke. However, after darkness fell the oil lamps began to fade and one of the students yelled at the servant, "The lamps need filling." The second student, upon hearing his friend speak, said, "Shhhh! We're supposed to be quiet!" Whereupon the third student scolded, "You idiots, what did you have to say anything for?" "I'm not saying a word," said the fourth student, gloating.[62]

In this chapter we will be talking about silence. Although much of what we reliably know about it results from the higher-order verbal abstractions of scientists, the process level of events, represented by the parabola, is not words. It exists on the silent level. Our experience, represented on the object level by the circle, also is not words. When you stub your toe, whatever you *say* it 'is', is not it! When you feel warmth, whatever the source, whatever you *say* it is, is not it.

Turning Down the Volume

We live and experience our lives on the silent, "unspeakable", non-verbal level of existence, although it seems that we are endlessly talking to ourselves. (For the moment we are putting aside the fact that our words, in some sense, also exist on the silent level, since everything that occurs is included in the parabola.) This self-talk, if intensional, can prevent us from functioning well. If we talk to ourselves extensionally, we can help ourselves to get in better touch with what is happening within and around us.

Eventually, however, a large part of living extensionally involves learning to turn down and turn off the volume of the words inside our heads. So an important part of GS training involves practice looking, listening, tasting, 'feeling', etc., at the silent, unspeakable level. We want to convey an attitude towards living that involves awareness of ourselves as organisms-as-wholes-in-environments.

This comes as a surprise to some people who come to general-semantics classes expecting simply to learn more about language use and "semantics", or the 'meanings' of words. They learn, however, as you are learning, that as evaluators we mainly transact with words, symbols and other events in terms of their significance or *'meanings' to us* and these 'meanings' that we make, these evaluations inside each one of us, *are not verbal*—not even 'verbal meanings'.

What do you do when you walk by a bakery? Observe what other people do. What non-verbal differences can you note between walking by a bakery and walking by a drug store, for example?

Facial expression, tone of voice, 'body' posture all reflect 'meanings' beyond the words that we hear. Such so-called 'body' language expresses the non-verbal thinking-feeling of each of us. Charlotte Schuchardt Read described a cartoon that Korzybski used which showed a drill sergeant berating a recruit: "Wipe that opinion off your face!"

These non-verbal behaviors not only convey 'meanings' to others, but to ourselves as well. Part of "talking to yourself" involves the tensions you experience, the habitual ways you perform tasks, the postural attitudes you bring to situations. You not only smile with happiness, but can create a good mood by smiling.

We will be focusing on several aspects of "turning down the volume" in this chapter.

Contemplating

Charlotte noted an attitude of contemplation as "the *sine qua non* of Korzybski's discipline."[63] This relates to his fundamental observation of structure as the only content of knowledge, discussed in Chapter 6. As Korzybski wrote,

> There is a tremendous difference between 'thinking' in verbal terms, and 'contemplating', inwardly silent, on non-verbal levels, and then searching for the proper structure of language to fit the supposedly discovered structure of the silent processes that modern science tries to find. If we 'think' *verbally*, we act as biased observers and project onto the silent levels the structure of the language we use, and so remain in our rut of old orientations, making keen, unbiased, observations and creative work well-nigh impossible. In contrast, when we 'think' without words, or in

pictures (which involve structure and therefore relations), we may discover new aspects and relations on silent levels, and so may produce important theoretical results between the two levels, silent and verbal. Practically all important advances are made that way.[64]

By learning how to contemplate non-verbally, we can prepare ourselves to behave scientifically, or extensionally. Freeing ourselves as much as possible from our beliefs about what we "should" or expect to see, we can become better observers as we test our higher-order abstractions.

Perhaps few of us are concerned, as was Korzybski, with building general systems of evaluation. However, most of us are concerned with building better ways of evaluating, with improving the quality of our lives. We often recognize that this quality involves some sense of a vast 'something' that we cannot put into words but that somehow connects us with our environments.

Many disciplines and philosophies touch on this. For example, Zen practices and other forms of meditation, hypnosis, "healing" practices, etc., point people toward experiencing such connections.

Creative work involves an openness to these connections. Aesthetic appreciation of music, art, dance, literature, 'nature', etc., involves an ability to connect non-verbally with our environments, internal and external.

With GS, we seek to encourage such contemplation and so greater creativity, aesthetic appreciation, sense of well-being, etc. We also seek to connect such contemplation with our higher-order verbal evaluating, in recognition of the inevitable connections between silent-level and verbal-level functioning. We seek, as expressed by Charlotte Read, to "<u>feel</u> ourselves as time-binders, considering 'time-binding' not just intellectually but as participating in the human experience of millenniums."[65]

Semantic (Evaluational) Relaxation

Our ability to contemplate on non-verbal levels comprises "a first requirement for learning to be conscious of abstracting".[66] Developing greater awareness of the non-verbal world can stimulate us to notice differences between the changing territories of life and our perceptual and verbal maps of them. Attention to our own non-verbal functioning can help us to achieve a greater sense of our own roles as map-makers. We thus emphasize non-verbal work as an important aspect of GS training.

Korzybski, along with his co-workers (primarily Charlotte Schuchardt Read), developed a practice he called "semantic relaxation" which was taught at his seminars. This semantic (evaluational) relaxation involved actually handling one's muscles and sensing the degree of tension, softness, hardness, etc., in them. Korzybski correlated increased muscular tension with defensiveness, 'emotional' tension and the readiness to jump to conclusions. Thus, by relaxing these tensions, he conjectured that people could become more open to their experiences, better able to take in and evaluate information.

Charlotte (and then Bruce) later led GS classes in non-verbal sensing, including listening, seeing, touching, moving, etc., incorporating the teachings of Charlotte's teacher Charlotte Selver. This work, which Selver labeled "sensory awareness", is based on the work of Selver's teacher Elsa Gindler (positive time-binding in action) and has profound connections to GS.

Sensory Awareness

Gindler taught physical education in Germany in the first part of the twentieth century. When she contracted tuberculosis, she had little money and no effective medical treatment available to her. She did have some confidence that by observing herself, how she breathed and functioned, she might improve her health.

She found that when she could get out of her own way, remain present here and now, and keep her attention on the actual processes of breathing and moving, she could allow what she needed for healing to take place. Some time later, when she encountered her doctor on the street, he seemed surprised that she was still alive. Indeed Gindler lived until 1961 and taught others, including Selver, this unique form of psycho-physical education.[67]

The Gindler work as taught by Selver and Read clearly embodies the notion of silence on the unspeakable level. With verbal and non-verbal guidance, attention is directed through questions and experiments to discover and observe what is going on in and around us. We learn to sense our organism-as-a-whole-in-environments connections by learning to stay in the present.

We would like to give you a taste of sensory awareness experiences, of staying in the present. So, enough explanation for now—time to get the flavor. As you read the following, allow yourself time to observe and respond:

What are you doing right now? As you read these words let yourself become aware of how you are sitting or lying down or standing...

How can you allow yourself to feel the support of what holds you up?

How much do you need to hold yourself up?

Where do you feel unnecessary tensions?

Do you feel tension in your jaw?

In your face?

Where do you feel ease?

How clearly can you feel yourself breathing?

Many events are occurring inside and outside your skin right now. Can you allow yourself non-verbally to experience these activities? When you focus unnecessarily on labeling and explaining, you may miss something important going on in and around you.

Listen to whatever sounds come to you right now... Do you find yourself labeling what you hear? Listen again and this time if you begin to label sounds just notice that you are doing it and allow yourself to come back to the sound again.

Touch the cloth of your clothes. Notice the sensations in your fingers, your hands. Allow the sensations to travel where they will. Move to a different part of your clothes. Notice any differences in sensations.

Choose something to look at. Without words, take in what comes to your eyes. Continue looking; what else comes to you?

Get up and walk around. Sense the movement of your feet and legs, the movement of your arms, the shifts in your torso.

Consider the sounds, sights, aromas around you as structures to explore. Pick an 'object' such as a stone or a pencil. Examine it closely, silently, for several minutes. Use 'all' of your senses: see, hear, touch, smell, taste, move it. How well can you do this without labeling or describing?

You may find that, like the Zen students, you quickly fall into speech, perhaps talking to yourself about something else. At such times it seems easy to scold yourself for not performing the task 'correctly'. When you practice such experiments, you may also find yourself, as we sometimes have, congratulating yourself verbally for remaining on the non-verbal level. If you find yourself doing these things, just notice it and go on. With practice, you'll find it easier to stay focused on the non-verbal level.

You may have noticed that we used the word "allow" in some of our suggestions for non-verbal awareness. Part of giving up "shoulds" and other kinds of higher-order abstractions involves allowing ourselves to experience whatever we're experiencing at the moment, accepting what we find.

People who work with us sometimes object that they want to change, not accept themselves as they presently function. However, as Gindler discovered, we find that people benefit from allowing themselves to experience whatever is occurring in the moment in any aspect of their organisms-as-wholes-in-environments. Positive changes can occur much more easily when we're not fighting what we experience.

As a simple example, we note how we use this approach ourselves for foot and leg cramps. We find that when we allow ourselves to focus on the sensations, noticing with "interest" (and varying degrees of difficulty) *how* the 'pain' 'feels', *how* the muscles twist...the cramp may disappear.

Focusing on process, on the means whereby something happens, leads to greater control over this and future happenings.

The Means Whereby

The Alexander Technique, which Bruce incorporates into his work, provides a good example of an educational discipline developed independently of GS that demonstrates, with its focus on silent-level experiencing, an extensional approach to improving human functioning.

Starting out as an actor, F. M. Alexander began to get hoarse and lose his voice during performances. Standard treatments provided only temporary relief. Like Gindler, he decided to observe himself and discovered that the tensions he created when he spoke were responsible for his problems. He explored his posture-movement habits in detail and discovered how to correct his speech problems. Subsequently, he developed an approach to helping people become more aware of and improve how they use themselves in their everyday activities. A central aspect of this approach involves developing greater awareness of what Alexander called "the means whereby" we do things.[68]

He noted that people tend to focus on the ends or goals of an activity: to speak in public, sit down, stand up, etc. Perhaps you can, in your usual way, get up and then sit down again now. Do it. Quite likely, in doing this you focused your attention on where you wanted to end up (and then down). When we do this, we tend to follow habitual patterns.

Attending to the "means whereby" of an activity involves focusing on *how* you get up and down, etc. By extensionally staying with the process, you can learn how to do things with less strain and greater ease.

Many people seek to improve their 'posture'. They do this by holding themselves according to their image of good posture. They start with some map of what they are supposed to do (the goal) and then impose it on themselves. In other words, they reverse the 'natural' order of abstracting.

In order to permit constructive change to occur, we must instead behave extensionally, as Alexander did. So first we observe what in fact we are doing with ourselves here and now on the silent level when we sit, stand, walk, garden, make the bed, etc. Then we can describe what we observe, make inferences, etc., and test them.

In this way we can begin to experiment with changing what we do. As you might guess, this extensional, experiential approach to changing posture-movement habits provides a model for dealing with other habits and skills as well.

Challenging Assumptions Non-Verbally

We can become aware of assumptions as we spend some time on the silent level. As Korzybski noted, we carry tensions organismically which reflect attitudes, beliefs, expectations, etc. As you practice non-verbal awareness, you can begin to notice differences in what you sense as you approach different situations. These differences reflect non-verbal and verbal aspects of your evaluating.

We also can use non-verbal awareness to change our assumptions. Eloise Ristad described how she and others tend to keep their eyes on the ground right in front of themselves when hiking. This behavior suggests an assumption that such close vigilance is required to prevent tripping and falling.

She decided to challenge this assumption by experimenting non-verbally with another way:

> I was curious about how many times I actually needed to look down in the next thirty or forty feet, and decided that my priority would be to see and sense as much as I could around me. So, letting my feet risk a little, I let my eyes drink in the scene around me. I found I had missed much of the beauty surrounding me... As I allowed a soft easy taking-in of the trail ahead, I found I seldom needed to lower my eyes to the spot just ahead of my feet. That spot became part of an overall awareness of my surroundings, and I found, to my surprise, that my feet usually knew precisely where to go, how to adjust to the tilt of a rock...when I indulged my eyes, my other senses came to life also, bringing a sense of ease to my whole body... Occasionally my eyes knew instinctively that they needed to double-check an obstacle, and did so in a split second. Then they went back to the visual pleasures of cumulus clouds nudging mountain peaks...[69]

In sum, developing non-verbal awareness gives us increased flexibility to be present and to respond more appropriately to what is occurring. As we let go of unnecessary assumptions and tensions and focus on the means whereby we function, we can avoid some obstacles, adjust to others, and enjoy life more fully. Coming to our senses allows us to behave uncommonly sensibly.

In focusing on becoming more aware of the silent, unspeakable levels, we do not intend to put down or leave out language. Our ability to use words seems central to what makes us human. And it always involves non-verbal aspects. Words exist, in their own right, on the silent level. And fully listening to others requires getting quiet inside, taking in aspects of language such as tone, gesture, etc. We can similarly listen to our own talk, including observing the internal talk that no one else can hear. And we can savor the sensual quality and play of poetry, drama, etc.

In addition, in order to develop uncommon sense, we want to understand how we can *use* words and not get 'used' by them. Do our words and other symbols create screens that blind us? Can our language point us towards and help us deal with the silent, unspeakable and unlabeled world in which we live and which includes ourselves?

Applications

1. (a) Write down a description of a sunset from memory.

   (b) Observe sunsets several times, without talking to yourself or others. Afterwards, write down what you saw.

   (c) Compare the above descriptions.

2. Silently observe grass for 15 to 30 minutes. Describe what you saw.

3. Take about 15 minutes outdoors. Focus on the sounds that come to you. Listen for the structure (differences and changes in pitch, loudness, complexity, relationships, etc.) of those sounds.

4. (a) Observe something without words.

   (b) Talk to yourself deliberately.

   (c) Return to silent observation.

5. During your next meal, spend some time silently allowing yourself to notice the flavors of your food.

6. How do these experiments help you to work on your personal concerns?

Chapter 9

Verbal Awareness

...it would be very unlikely for unlikely events not to occur. If you don't specify a predicted event precisely, there are an indeterminate number of ways for an event of that general kind to take place.

John Allen Paulos[70]

We often live, feel happy or unhappy, by what actually amounts to a definition, *and not by the empirical, individual facts less coloured by semantic [evaluational] factors.*

Alfred Korzybski[71]

So we move on to levels of language, our human dimension. We want to emphasize at the start of this discussion that we can't use language without also experiencing non-verbally. As you create words to describe and evaluate your experiences, that creation involves the non-verbal workings of your nervous system. These words you're reading are creations of our nervous systems and don't take on 'meaning' until sensed and evaluated by your nervous system. Your understanding of what you read may be influenced by where and how you sit and when and what you last ate. So let's remember, as we talk about language we're talking about *neuro*-linguistics; the event and object levels of our abstracting always accompany us.

In the last chapter we continued our discussion of the process of abstracting by focusing on experiencing on the silent level. As we move to verbal levels, we're dealing with the levels of description (statements of 'fact'), inferences, generalizations, hypotheses, theories, etc. These levels represent our ability to talk about our silent-level experiencing and to talk about our talking. Our examination of these levels will prepare the way for later chapters in which we'll be discussing particular ways to improve our use of language.

In the Dark

Korzybski once told a story from the European anti-Hitler underground:

> ...In a railroad compartment an American grandmother with her young and attractive granddaughter, a Romanian officer, and a Nazi officer were the only occupants. The train was passing through a dark tunnel, and all that was heard was a loud kiss and a vigorous slap."

What do you 'think' happened during the passage through the tunnel? What other possibilities can you come up with? How confident and certain do you feel about these possibilities?

These questions address the issue of how we learn to distinguish among verbal levels, particularly between statements of 'fact' and other higher-order abstractions. What do we need to take into account as we work towards abstracting more consciously and effectively?

To return to our cliff-hanger (or should we say tunnel-tussle), Korzybski continued:

> After the train emerged from the tunnel, nobody spoke, but the grandmother was saying to herself, "What a fine girl I have raised. She will take care of herself. I am proud of her." The granddaughter was saying to herself, "Well, grandmother is old enough not to mind a little kiss. Besides, the fellows are nice. I'm surprised what a hard wallop grandmother has." The Nazi officer was meditating, "How clever those Romanians are! They steal a kiss and have the other fellow slapped." The Romanian officer was chuckling to himself, "How smart I am! I kissed my own hand and slapped the Nazi."[72]

How close did you come to what happened? On what were you basing your response? What facts did you have? What facts did the four people on the train have?

We base most of our conclusions on varying degrees of incomplete information. However, because we don't often experience ourselves as living in the dark, we often fail to recognize the limits on the facts available to us.

We also often view inferences (what we conclude is going on) as 'facts' and act on that basis. Can you imagine grandmother congratulating her granddaughter later (and perhaps trusting her without adequately preparing her further to take care of herself)? Can you imagine the granddaughter inappropriately changing her understanding of her grandmother? What consequences might occur for the officers?

The confusion of factual statements and inferences can have consequences ranging from funny to tragic. We can enjoy the fun but had best prepare ourselves so we avoid or minimize the tragic. Avoiding and undoing such confusion can take you a long way towards consciousness of abstracting.

Facts and Inferences

Let's shed some light on the distinguishing features of the levels of statements of fact and inference. For the purposes of this discussion, we can view any evaluating we do beyond facts as making inferences—lower-order inferences and higher-order inferences. Thus with inferences we're considering what people call assumptions, interpretations, conclusions, generalizations, hypotheses, guesses, hunches, judgments, beliefs, etc.

Irving J. Lee made the following distinctions:[73]

Statements of fact (description):
1. Must be based on observables, occurring in the present or the past.
2. Can get verified through other observations, preferably made by other observers.
3. Come close to certainty.

Statements of inference:
1. Can refer to occurrences in the present, past or future.
2. Go beyond what we can observe and verify.
3. Involve degrees of probability.

Some aspects of Lee's distinctions warrant further consideration. As discussed below, we prefer to talk of higher degrees of probability rather than 'close to certainty'.

We want to emphasize that, since as of this date we can't observe the future, *nothing* about the future can be considered as fact. We may assume with a fair degree of certainty that in a few hours the sky will turn dark and some hours later it will turn light again. However, even our future relation to the sun involves only a high degree of probability. We *do not know* anything about the future with the certainty of a statement of fact.

We all can and do make statements to ourselves and others about our internal processes. These statements may represent more or less accurate descriptions of those processes, and only the individuals themselves can evaluate the degree of accuracy.

We cannot verify other people's internal processes, only what people say about them. If someone reports to me that you said you feel sad, I can verify this by asking you. However, I cannot verify the feeling itself. I thus have a choice as to how trustworthy I find your report. Based on my experiences with you, my observations of your behavior, etc., I make an inference about this. I do best to recognize this as an inference.

Fact-Inference Continuum

We find it important to note that Korzybski developed the structural differential as a teaching tool. As a teaching tool, we find it helpful to act sometimes as if we can make sharp distinctions among the levels. However, as we've already noted, even our silent-level experiences represent "perceptual bets" and as such can be considered as inferences. Because all of our knowledge represents the incomplete abstracting of a fallible nervous system, in some ways all levels of abstracting can be considered as inferences.

So when we're distinguishing facts from other inferences we're involved with degrees of probability. How do we differentiate a factual statement's closeness to certainty from an inferential statement's degrees of probability? We don't in any absolute sense. Therefore, as Kenneth Johnson suggested, we prefer to view these processes on a continuum, not as sharp categories. The continuum looks like this.

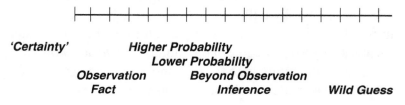

Figure 9-1 Fact-Inference Continuum

The degree and kind of information we need to determine something as a fact varies. At a minimum, we do best to stay with publicly observable occurrences in the past or present when we consider something as close to certain, as representing a fact.

You can note that we list nothing under 'certainty' in the above continuum. Any guesses as to the reasons? Most of you probably have inferred correctly that we doubt whether anything qualifies as absolutely certain. We suggest you also evaluate in this way.

Converging Inferences

How can we increase our degree of 'certainty'? Consider the following newspaper story.[74]

> When the trashmen told a Woodlawn Beach man early yesterday that they would be back to pick up his garbage, the resident apparently didn't believe them ...the man allegedly [notice the caution in expressing what wasn't observed by the reporter] set off in his 1977 green Lincoln Continental to make sure they did. He took along a pistol too, the police said later. And by the time the chase was over, the trash truck allegedly had been slammed by the Lincoln and shot at twice by the Woodlawn Beach man. The Lincoln, in turn, had been rammed by the trash truck and pushed off the side of the road as the trashmen tried to flee for safety...

Of course, we can only make inferences about this situation: *our* only facts involve the words we read in our newspaper; *your* only facts involve the words you read on this page. So let's infer.

What facts about this seem highly probable? We would say that it seems highly probable that the events occurred somewhat as reported and that we know very little about the man's and the trashmen's motivation. We infer that the man's behavior represented an unreasonable response, regardless of the circumstances (the report mentions alcohol as a factor in the incident; we would add taking along a pistol as another).

Let's suppose that the man didn't believe that the trashmen would be back. We can recognize this as an inference on his part, because he's predicting something in the future.

What degree of probability might this inference have? He seemed to act as if it had a high degree of probability. What-might lead to an expectation of a high degree of probability that the trashmen wouldn't come back? Perhaps the man had had many prior experiences of this kind of commitment not getting fulfilled. Perhaps his neighbors had reported many of these kinds of experiences. Perhaps he had read about such incidents in his local paper. Perhaps he knew that local politicians were considering what to do about inconsistent trash pick-up. Each of these varied sources of information would make his prediction somewhat more probable (although none would excuse his behavior).

We call such combinations of inferences CONVERGING INFERENCES. With a higher number of converging inferences we can place more confidence in our predictions. As we noted, in part this represents the method of science. However, as in science, we want to look for evidence which might contradict our inferences as well as support them.

Thus our Woodlawn Beach man, even with converging inferences about unreliability of trash pick-up, would have done well to consider how often the trashmen *did* return as promised. He would also have done well to recognize that any potential situation involves a new situation—about which we don't have facts.

We cannot blithely assume that our expectations about the future represent Truth with a capital T. While our past experiences can help us prepare for the future, we do best by considering the following. Remember the example in Chapter 2 of how you formed generalizations (theories) about apples when you were growing up. We noted then the importance of checking our generalizations against our experiences. However many experiences we have had with what we call apples, when we come to a new 'object' which resembles an apple, we do best by recognizing that this represents a new situation. We can call our accumulated past experiences "n"; then the new experience becomes "n + 1". Much of using GS involves recognizing how we accumulate and can best evaluate our "n" experiences and how we can best prepare for the "n + 1", remembering that "n + 1" is not the same as "n".

Do you wonder what happened to the man's trash? As reported, "The trashmen didn't have time to go back for it." Do you imagine that the man might now feel justified in his expectation that they wouldn't return? How often do we help create the situations we expect and then evaluate the turn of events as 'proof' that we evaluated correctly?

Observations-Descriptions-Facts-Inferences

In recognizing that even all so-called statements of fact-represent lower-level inferences, we can appreciate the importance of close observation in order to feel closer to certainty. We can appreciate that accumulating close observations over time also represents a development of converging inferences. The closer we stay to these observations, and the more accurately we describe them, the closer we get to facts.

Let's consider an example of what we view as helpful evaluating in using observation and description to check inferences and get out of muddles. Dr. Sidney Rosen reported on the following case as told by Milton Erickson, M.D., a psychiatrist who used hypnosis in his work.[75]

> A patient came to me and said, "I've lived in Phoenix for the past fifteen years and I have hated every moment of those fifteen years. My husband has offered me a vacation in Flagstaff. I hate Phoenix so much, but I have refused to go to Flagstaff. I prefer to stay in Phoenix and to *hate* being in Phoenix."
>
> So I told her, while she was in a trance, that she would be curious about hating Phoenix and about why she punished herself so much. That should be a very *big* curiosity. "And

there is another thing to be curious about—and very, very curious about. If you go to Flagstaff for a week, you will see, very unexpectedly, a flash of color." As long as she had a big curiosity about hating Phoenix, she could develop an *equally* large curiosity, just as compelling, to find out what that flash of color would be in Flagstaff.

She went to Flagstaff for a week, but stayed a month. What flash of color did she see? I had none in mind. I just wanted her to be curious. And when she saw that flash of color, she was so elated that she remained a whole month in Flagstaff. That flash of color was a redheaded wood-pecker flying past an evergreen tree. This woman usually spends her summer in Flagstaff now, but she also has gone to the East Coast to see the color *there*. She has gone to Tucson, to see a flash of color. She has gone to Europe, to see a flash of color. And my statement that she would see a flash of color was based only upon the fact that you have to see a lot of things that ordinarily *you* don't see. And I wanted her to *keep looking*. And she would *find something* to translate into my words.

This woman came to Erickson living her life by definition: "Phoenix is a hateful place. I hate Phoenix. I have to stay in the place I hate." We can infer, given these definitions, that she didn't see much possibility of enjoyment.

Erickson gave her the task of observing, of acting curious about what she might see. He didn't say, in this abbreviated report, how she described her experiences to him, although she apparently reported on a flash of red against green, namely a redheaded woodpecker against evergreen tree.

These experiences, and descriptions, apparently enabled her to redefine her situation and continue her curiosity for new flashes. She might also (and perhaps did) reevaluate her hatred of Phoenix, perhaps identifying some times and circumstances when she found it less than hateful. Perhaps flashes of color appeared there too. Perhaps her 'truth' about Phoenix changed.

We hope you evaluate this as an example of taking a scientific approach in everyday life. We hope you recognize the advantages of checking out your definitions and not living by them alone. We hope you recognize the importance of accurately describing what you experience, and then basing your inferences on those descriptions.

We also have options about the inferences we make from specific circumstances accurately described. Suppose you plant a vegetable garden and you notice that the leaves of the squash plant have turned yellow, the stems look hollow, the squash never get bigger than one inch long. We can say that this represents a description of that part of your garden. Would you infer this as a failure? Consider the following report about a gardener:

> She likes to think of herself as a scientist, someone who, as she says, "tries something in order to see what happens." Curiosity is a large part of what keeps her gardening, and she is unafraid to try something if it has even the slightest chance of working. "You can say that something has failed, or you can say it came out differently than you wanted it to," she states optimistically, adding that an idea can always be adapted in order to make it work.[76]

Since your choice of inferences feeds back to influence your later experiences, you will benefit from learning how to evaluate your inferential statements more carefully, and how to change them to help create a more positive future.

What We Can Determine: Degrees of Probability

One aspect of determining facts involves determining the degree of truth in any situation. We've touched on this in our discussion of reports of internal processes and the three stories presented here. Common sense suggests that when we can state 'facts' we have the 'truth'. However, we've observed that even so-called statements of fact involve complex factors and a degree of uncertainty. Using uncommon sense, we accept Stuart Mayper's dictum: "No facts are simple." Perhaps the best we can do is view so-called factual statements as "truish".

Common sense also suggests that we can determine most statements as either true or false. We usually grow up in environments which encourage us to give the "right" answers and to avoid looking like we don't know the facts. Therefore we often want to avoid saying, "I don't know," or "I don't know what you 'mean'," or "I'm not sure what I 'mean'," or "I don't have enough information," or "Maybe."

Using uncommon sense, we recognize that fewer statements than many of us think fall into the realm of the descriptive, or factual, as we've defined it, i.e., statements about public, observable, verifiable events occurring in the past or present. Most of our statements go beyond this, into the realm of the inferential.

Descriptive, factual statements can ideally be directly determined as true or false. When we have a descriptive statement, we can compare it to what it describes. If the description fits what is described, we can label it as true. If the description contradicts or in any way doesn't fit what is described, we can label it as false. (In practice a 'descriptive' statement may combine true, false and inferred elements, making what's 'true'and 'false' more fuzzy.)

What about statements of inference? These statements, which go beyond what can be observed, appear more indeterminate than descriptions. We can't as easily determine them as either true or false, either because we may not have enough information or because we may not know what the statement 'means' in sufficient detail to determine its 'truth'. We can view such statements as variables which can have greater or lesser probability and testability. About statements of inference we often do best to say, "I don't know," or "I don't have enough information," or "I don't know what you or I 'mean'," or "Maybe."

When we use the uncommon sense of acknowledging the limits of our inferential statements, we allow ourselves to ask, "What do you 'mean'?" "What do I 'mean'?" "How do we know?" "How can we find out more?" These questions can lead us toward more descriptive statements, which we might then be able to evaluate as true or false. We hope you recognize this, too, as part of a scientific attitude.

Let's consider some examples from the story about the train. Using the information in the story, we'll evaluate each statement below as true (T), false (F), or indeterminate (?). We use a "?" to indicate that more information is needed. You can note how you evaluate each statement before you read our discussion. You can look back at the story.

1. Someone spoke after the train came out of the tunnel.

2. Grandmother acted as the girl's mother.

3. The officers were men.

4. Four people sat in a railroad compartment.

5. The Romanian officer was chuckling to himself.

6. The story is a good illustration.

We evaluate Statement 1 as false, since the story directly states that nobody spoke, and Statement 1 contradicts that.

We evaluate Statement 2 as indeterminate. While the story states Grandmother's thought that she raised the girl, we don't have enough information to know if she functioned fully and solely as her mother.

We evaluate Statement 3 as indeterminate although truish (most likely 'true'), since the girl refers to "The fellows". We say "truish" and not 'true' because it's possible that the girl was using "fellows" to refer to people in general, just as a mixed group may be referred to as "you guys".

We evaluate Statement 4 as indeterminate, since some or all of the people could have been standing or lying down.

We evaluate Statement 5 as true, since the words of the statement exactly match, or map, the words of the story, or territory.

We evaluate Statement 6 as indeterminate, because, as stated, we don't know what "good" 'means'. We'd want to ask, "What do you mean by 'good'? Good for what? Good when?" etc.

You'll have more opportunity to practice sorting out statements like these in the **Applications** section of this chapter.

More about Less, Less about More

As we've noted, abstracting involves a process of leaving out and leaving in. At each higher level, we've necessarily left out details from lower levels. We can say that at lower levels we have more details about particular individual items. At the descriptive level, we can describe in detail, for example, a redheaded woodpecker or an evergreen tree. We're not describing other woodpeckers or trees. At the lowest levels, we're dealing with unique individuals, no two identical. We're focusing on differences. We can say we're including more detail about less items.

As indicated by Erickson, these items can be viewed as "flashes of color", a higher-order abstraction. Many items might fit this higher-order abstraction. Indeed, the woman he worked with found "flashes of color" in many locations.

As indicated by Erickson, he could feel quite certain that the woman would see (we can infer she wasn't blind) "a lot of things". When we look for "things", we're at yet a higher level of abstraction, which includes still more items than "flashes of color". "Things" include "flashes of color", which in turn include woodpeckers and trees, which in turn include particular woodpeckers and trees. We can say we're including more items in less detail.

As we add items, we're focusing on similarities, from which we form our categories. So we can say that we're adding more about some similarities we've derived. In later chapters we'll be returning to issues related to categories.

In discussing "less about more," that is, what we're adding as we get to higher levels of abstraction, we want to emphasize the important creative aspects of these higher levels. As we've noted, they form the foundation of modern scientific knowledge. These levels represent our ability to talk about our talking, to evaluate our evaluating, to generalize and form theories.

We noted the value of converging inferences. In complex situations, these can give us greater security than any single observation. Also, these higher-level abstractions become part of, and enrich, the subsequent territories from which we then abstract.

The title of Ken Johnson's book *Thinking Creatically*[77] indicates the GS view about lower-order and higher-order abstractions. We value the *creati*vity of higher-order abstractions, as checked out cri*tically* against lower-order abstractions.

We've noted in this chapter the importance of how we phrase our statements and responses. In the next chapter, we consider these and other issues as we examine the structure of our language.

Applications

1. Consider an important decision you've made. What additional information might you have found helpful? Was it potentially obtainable at the time? If so, how might you have become aware of it and obtained it?

2. Read a magazine or newspaper article. Determine each statement as representing a statement of fact or a statement of inference. What proportion of each do you find? Pick a different magazine or newspaper and repeat these steps. Any differences in proportion?

3. Compare two news stories on the 'same' event or situation. What facts do you find in each? What inferences? How do you evaluate the similarities and differences? What conclusions can you draw?

4. What do you feel certain of? (Fess up – to yourself, at least. We nigh always feel certain of something.) How do you know?

5. How do you define yourself? Based on what evidence? How have converging inferences influenced this definition?

6. Evaluate the following statements as True (T), False (F), or Indeterminate (?).

> The first sentence in this chapter says, "So we move on to levels of language, our human dimension."
>
> This book is about manufacturing computers.
>
> My friend will enjoy the stories in this book.
>
> Susan and Bruce have a garden.
>
> Alfred Korzybski claims, "The map is the territory."
>
> Semmelweis was a good physician.
>
> Assumptions get us into trouble.
>
> Using science, we can prove our points.
>
> All swans are white.
>
> We can be objective when we use science.
>
> Snake meat makes people sick.

Consider what information you'd need to make the "indeterminate" statements more probably true or false. We discuss our evaluations of these statements in the Notes for this chapter.[78]

7. How do these experiments and questions help you to work on your personal concerns?

Chapter 10

The Structure of Language

Our choicest plans
have fallen through,
Our airiest castles
tumbled over,
Because of lines
we neatly drew
And later neatly
stumbled over.

Piet Hein[79]

Here we come across a tremendous fact; namely, that a language, any language, has at its bottom certain metaphysics, which ascribe, consciously or unconsciously, some sort of structure to this world...We do not realize what tremendous power the structure of an habitual language has. It is not an exaggeration to say that it enslaves us through the mechanism of s.r [semantic (evaluational) reaction(s)] and the structure which a language exhibits, and impresses upon us unconsciously, is automatically projected upon the world around us.

Alfred Korzybski[80]

In the **Applications** section of the chapter on non-verbal awareness, we asked you to experiment with noting the structure of sounds around you. When we do this at seminar-workshops, we sometimes get the following kinds of responses. Some people hear the sounds as symphonies, focusing on relationships and rhythms; some people hear them as isolated bits which dominate their attention, focusing on individual elements; some people hear other kinds of patterns. What did you hear?

We don't classify any of these ways as right or wrong, but recognize that our past experiences lead to certain ways of hearing and certain assumptions about sound. These assumptions influence how we hear the world. A "symphony" sounds different from isolated sounds. Next time you do this, listen deliberately for a symphony; for dominant individual sounds; for the pattern(s) you heard before.

Similarly, the structure of our language seems to influence how we direct our attention to whatever is going on and thus construct our experience, i.e., how we ongoingly abstract. What do we mean by "the structure of our language"? Among other things, this includes vocabulary (words); how we put words together to make sentences (grammar); and how we put sentences together to draw conclusions (logic). Our concern for language structure includes the communicators: how we allocate meanings as we express ourselves by means of mouth noises, marks on paper, etc., and attempt to understand and assess what others express. We can also look into how different language structures have developed over time, as well as how different languages differ in structure. And most central to the subject of this book, we can ask: What do all these structures have to do with how we humans behave, deal with difficulties, and relate to one another for better and worse?

Linguistic anthropologists such as Benjamin Lee Whorf and Edward Sapir studied the languages of different cultures. Their findings supported Korzybski's notions about the power of language structure. For example, we have one word for the white stuff that sometimes falls from the sky in cold weather, and we tend to simply evaluate in terms of whether or not it's snowing. We may modify the word snow with such adjectives as heavy, light, etc., and, after it's been on the ground for a while, as dirty or slushy, but one word generally suffices for our needs.

However, the Inuit (Eskimo) people have different needs in regard to snow, because of the severity of their winters. To survive those winters, they need to distinguish among many different kinds of snow. Reflecting this, the vocabulary of their language includes words for many different kinds of snow.[81] To what extent does the way both we and the Inuit talk not only reflect but influence our respective perceptions and related behavior?

As you may gather from the above discussion, we are not skiers; they also benefit from more words for snow than those of us who stay in by the fire. We've read the following terms that skiers use to differentiate what's under ski and thus help themselves adjust to the environment: mashed potatoes, windslab, corn snow, slush, powder, new-fallen powder, ego fluff powder, breakable crust, ice, frozen granular, crud.

Different occupations as well as hobbies often have particular vocabularies. What an outsider may call "jargon" provides important distinctions to those using the words. In what areas of your life do you have words that make more differentiations than others may make? How does this influence your perceptions and behavior?

In our discussion of structure, we pointed out the tendency we have to divide up the world into things and what they do. This results from the subject-predicate nature of Indo-European languages like English. A well-formed sentence in English requires a subject or noun (substantive) form and a predicate or verb form. Do we necessarily have to carve up the world this way?

Whorf, like Korzybski, believed not. He wrote:

> We are constantly reading into nature fictional acting entities, simply because our verbs must have substantives in front of them. We have to say 'It flashed' or 'A light flashed,' setting up an actor, 'it' or 'light,' to perform what we call an action, "to flash." Yet the flashing and the light are one and the same! The Hopi language reports the flash with a simple verb, rehpi: 'flash (occurred).' There is no division into subject and predicate, not even a suffix like -t of Latin tona-t 'it thunders.' Hopi can and does have verbs without subjects, a fact which may give that tongue potentialities, probably never to be developed, as a logical system for understanding some aspects of the universe.[82]

As we noted in Chapter 3, we function on the basis of certain unspoken assumptions which form our world view, or metaphysics. The structure of our language may reflect a central aspect of our metaphysics, which in the case of English includes certain assumptions about actors and actions requiring subjects and predicates. How might our world view differ if we spoke a language in which 'things' and 'what they do' co-existed within what Whorf proposed as "a more verblike concept but without the concealed premises of actor and action"?[83] What other kinds of assumptions are built into English? How have they been passed down to us in our rules of grammar and logic?

The Aristotelian Orientation

Aristotle (384-322 B.C.E.), a brilliant formulator of his time, observed the language structure of that time. From his observations he derived his logic, what came to be known as the "laws of thought". His influence remains far-reaching because his work was viewed not only as descriptive of the structure of Indo-European Greek, but also as prescriptive; not only the way things 'are', but the way they 'will and should be' for 'all' time.

Since the aristotelian language structure still dominates our language, let's take a look at what it involves.[84]

Aristotle's "laws of thought" involve three basic premises. He proposed that a thing is what it is: A is A. For example, "Facts are facts." "A fault is a fault." "An apple is an apple." (This is known as the premise of identity.)

He proposed that anything must either be a particular category or class of thing or not be that thing: Anything is either A or not-A. For example, "Something is either a fact or not a fact." "Something is either a fault or not a fault." "Something is either an apple or not an apple." (This is known as the premise of the excluded middle.)

He proposed that anything cannot both be a particular thing and not be that particular thing: Something cannot be both A and not-A. For example, "Something cannot both be a fact and not be a fact." "Something cannot both be a fault and not be a fault." "Something cannot both be an apple and not an apple." (This is known as the premise of non-contradiction.)

The "laws of thought" as metaphysical principles (structural assumptions) about the world seemed like common sense in Aristotle's time, before the microscopes and other instruments which enabled us to develop modern physical science. Aristotle's logic also reflected common sense before knowledge of other cultures and languages enabled us to develop modern social science. When we have only our senses to get our information, we see the world only at the macroscopic level, as described in Chapter 5, and miss a great deal. When we have only one culture and language which we consider 'correct', we see the world only from that restricted point of view. These limitations of our naive senses and unconscious cultural backgrounds still seem quite natural. As a result our 'common sense', reflected in aristotelian structural assumptions, ends up severely out-of-date.

This out-of-date common sense as we've noted, may lead us to sense certain "structures", and therefore assume them as correct; for example, when we look out at the horizon it looks as if the earth ends, which at one time led to assumptions of a flat earth. It may lead us to assume that things we can't sense, like germs, can't have effects. It may lead us to assume that qualities reside in things: "The rose is red." "The boy is lazy." It may lead us to assume that the way we and our culture categorize things is the way things are: "An apple is an apple." "Psychologists are psychologists." It may lead us to assume that if some*thing* happened or someone experienced some*thing*, some *thing* must exist to have caused the happening or experience: "My boss caused my failure." "Because I'm aware of reading these pages, I must have some 'thing', like a 'mind', causing that awareness." It may lead us to assume that 'things' are separate from what they do.

In sum, following the ARISTOTELIAN ORIENTATION leads us to view the world as static and unchanging. It leads us to assume we can know all. It leads us to assume our categories exist in the world and cannot be changed. It leads us to look for single causes for events. It leads us to evaluate in either/or terms. It leads us to a lack of awareness of our own evaluating process. This orientation so permeates our culture that for most people these ways of evaluating still seem like common sense.

However, just as we have gone beyond 19th century common sense regarding cleanliness, so also do we need to go beyond the common sense of Aristotle's time to develop uncommon sense in how we talk about our experiences. We need to go beyond Aristotle's orientation, so that our language reflects our current knowledge, which goes beyond our senses to the submicroscopic levels. We need to use higher orders of scientific abstracting, as well as our own non-verbal sensing. We imagine that Aristotle also would long ago have gone beyond his "laws of thought", using his brilliance to keep up with modern developments.

A Non-Aristotelian Orientation

In developing general semantics, Korzybski went beyond Aristotle. He took modern science as his "metaphysics" and formulated GS as a methodology to embody a NON-ARISTO-TELIAN ORIENTATION, which acknowledges the process world of constant change, the function of our nervous systems in our experiences of that process world, the complexity of issues in determining facts, etc., as we've already described. Korzybski's three basic non-aristotelian premises continue to reflect current knowledge, just as Aristotle's premises (taken as structural assumptions about the world) reflected what was current about 2300 years ago. "Non-aristotelian" in the korzybskian sense *does not* mean anti-aristotelian. In particular, we want to make clear that GS (not a 'logic' in the restricted formal sense of that term) does not reject aristotelian logic when appropriate. We do reject taking the aristotelian 'laws' of logic as metaphysical principles. However, we still find them useful when interpreted as rules for discourse under some circumstances of daily life and work. We discuss an example of this below, in the section labeled "Either/Or".

We also want you to note that Korzybski referred to GS as *a* non-aristotelian system, not *the* non-aristotelian system. He fully expected other non-aristotelian systems to be formulated (including new kinds of logic) to keep up with modern developments. In this, Korzybski seemed ahead of his time. We note in much of what we read today a movement toward formulating things in non-aristotelian terms. For example, the field of "fuzzy logic", developed by Lotfi Zadeh, professor emeritus of electrical engineering and computer science at the University of California at Berkeley, replaces sharp exclusion or inclusion in a category with degrees of exclusion/inclusion. Fuzzy logic can be used to formulate in a mathematically exact manner how something *can* be considered both A and not-A. It has been successfully applied in designing machine control systems.[85]

Let's return to the basic general-semantics premises and compare them to the aristotelian premises.

Aristotelian	**Non-aristotelian**
A *is* A. (Identity)	"A map *is not* the territory." (Non-identity)
Anything is *either* A or not A. (Excluded middle)	"A map covers *not all* the territory. (Non-Allness)
Something *cannot be both* A and not-A. (Non-contradiction)	"A map is self-reflexive."[86] (Self-reflexiveness)

While the premises of the two systems do not strictly parallel each other, we can usefully make links between them. Let's start with the first premise of each system, analyzing "A is A" in general-semantics terms.

We can note that, as written on the paper, the second "A" differs from the first "A" in location, and at submicroscopic and microscopic levels they can be assumed to differ, even if very slightly, in quantity of ink, etc. Further, the second "A" was written slightly later than the first "A". We could say that the second "A" constitutes a map of the territory of the first "A"—and *that* map is not the territory. Whatever we say something is, is not it.

While these may seem like trivial points, when we consider "A" as a variable which can be assigned many 'meanings'—for example, apple, house, Bruce, Susan, you, your friend, student, politician, etc.—the issues involved can have serious consequences. Consider the tragedies associated with formulating that 'Serbs' are 'Serbs', 'Croats' are 'Croats', 'Muslims' are 'Muslims'. In this and other chapters we examine these issues.

We can note that in each system, premises 2 and 3 derive from the first premise. If "A is A", then anything must be either A or not-A, and something cannot be both. If "a map is not the territory", then a map cannot cover all the territory and maps can be made of maps.

Non-Identity

Thus, just as identity serves as the center of the aristotelian orientation, non-identity serves as the center of the non-aristotelian orientation of Korzybski. As a basic premise, we assume that *no* two individuals (objects, events, reactions, etc.) are identical (absolutely the same in all aspects). Similarly, *no* individual is even absolutely the same with itself from one moment to the next. Remember what Heraclitus said about stepping into the same river twice? And as we noted before, each map that we make of a prior territory is not the same as that prior territory. We noted that what we sense non-verbally, our perceptual mapping, is not 'what is'—what Bob Pula called "the naked it" of inferred process 'reality'. How does the recognition of non-identity influence how we behave verbally, that is, how we use language? How do we use language to indicate that what we say is not what 'is'? How do we use language to indicate that what we say is not all there 'is'? How do we use language to indicate that we can talk about our talking at different levels?

Non-Elementalism

As we've noted, from modern science we infer that we live in a process world. As we abstract non-verbally, we experience-create our 'perceptions' of 'things' from a kaleidoscopic flux of changing relations. As we speak, we name and describe these 'things', *which don't exist as we 'know' 'them' apart from our abstracting.* Yet when we name and describe these 'things' our language suggests their existence as separate entities, apart from how we get to 'know' 'them'.

In GS, we use the term ELEMENTALISM to label the neuro-evaluative process of *unconsciously* dividing up, separating, and isolating with our categories and words what doesn't actually exist so divided, separated, and isolated. The process may start before words in various forms of narrowed attention. Language use in general may structurally bias us towards further narrowing. Without awareness of these tendencies, we are likely to assume identity—and voila, we have elementalism. Without awareness, we will divide, separate and accept as isolated what does not exist in isolation, disregarding important relationships, ignoring context, etc. Confusing part for whole, we identify our resulting maps with the territory, our words with experiences, our experiences with 'the way things really are'.

Inherited aristotelian language structure further seems to encourage the elementalistic tendency to create static isolated elements out of the dynamic interrelated processes found in the world, which includes ourselves. We tend to project these static elements upon whatever we experience.

We already noted that we can talk about 'thinking' apart from 'feeling'. We can speak of 'minds' and 'bodies', 'structure' and 'function', 'physical' and 'mental', 'space' and 'time', 'organism' and 'environment'. We can speak of 'the unconscious'. We can act as if we can divorce 'actions' from 'consequences'.[87]

When we identify elementalistically, we then may look for 'minds' as if we can find 'them' as easily as we can find apples. We may look for 'the unconscious' rather than considering out-of-awareness processes. We may act without awareness and, perhaps, without concern for consequences of our actions.

NON-ELEMENTALISM involves recognizing and remedying this false-to-fact, static, isolating viewpoint. We seek to get as much of a sense of process and relations as possible into awareness and into our language. We've noted the importance of similarity of structure between and among levels of abstracting. Non-elementalism in language involves developing a similarity of structure between our words and the processes we're talking about. We've already noted some ways in which we do this, including using single quotes, hyphens and non-elementalistic terms. Other methods will be discussed in later chapters.

The "Ises"

Another aspect of non-identity involves the use of the verb "to be" in our language. As Korzybski said, "The little word 'to be' appears as a very peculiar word and is, perhaps, responsible for many human semantic [evaluational] difficulties."[88] In using various forms of this verb (is, am, are, were, will be, etc.) we can project false evaluations onto ourselves and others.

The word "is" plays a central role in the aristotelian major premises. As already noted, the aristotelian "A is A" suggests an identity, which Korzybski defined as "absolute sameness in all respects",[89] between two somethings. Yet we now know that we live in an ever-changing process world of unique individuals.

How can any two somethings be identical? Even if, to our eyes (brains), let us say, two apples look the 'same', what do you think would happen to this 'sameness' were we to look at them under a microscope? And very few 'objects' look exactly the same even to our eyes. When we thus use "is" we emphasize similarities and ignore differences. How about you? Are you the 'same' from moment-to-moment? No change at all? Of course not: you as an organism-as-a-whole-in-environments constantly change at the submicroscopic level. 'You' now are not exactly the same as 'you' yesterday or even a minute ago!

With a GS orientation, we clearly deny the aristotelian "ises". We state "A *is not* A." "The map *is not* the territory." A "territory" at space-time$_1$ is not that "territory" at space-time$_2$. A "map" at space- time$_1$ is not that "map" at space-time$_2$. An apple is not another apple. An apple is not 'itself' a moment later. We emphasized this in our discussion of the process of abstracting. Now we will examine in greater detail the role of "is" and other forms of the verb "to be" in how we use language.

This verb can be used in at least four ways. One way involves existence and location: "I am here and you are there." We have little problem with this use. Another way involves what is called an auxiliary use; in other words, it is used with another verb. We may say, "I am running," to indicate an ongoing activity. Or we may say "is called" and "is used", as we did two sentences ago (the passive). These auxiliary forms give us flexibility in our language and we have little problem with their use either (although the passive form, in not specifying the actor(s) can be used to obscure responsibility for actions).

Two other uses, however, can allow us to say things in a way that, strictly speaking, contradict what we know about how we abstract. Using "is" we can say, "This is a rose." "A rose is a rose." Susan can say, "I am a psychologist." This use (sometimes called the "is of identity") facilitates linking two nouns as if they are identical. Yet we know that at the event level no two roses are the same. We know that, while Susan trained as a psychologist, "psychologist" does not comprise her total identity, as the sentence may imply. We also know that "psychologist" can have different 'meanings'.

We have other ways of phrasing our sentences to avoid this 'is' and discourage identification. For example, we may say that "We call this a rose," to make explicit the fact that we have thus categorized it. We may say, "Rose$_1$ is not rose$_2$," and, if desired, describe aspects of each rose as we see it. Susan may say, "I work as a psychologist," suggesting this represents only part of her activities. Susan may say, "I use GS in my work," indicating that different psychologists work differently.

Using "is" we can also say, "The rose is red." "I am tall." "He is lazy." This use (called the "is of predication") links a noun and an adjective which modifies that noun. Using "is" in this way may suggest that redness is found in the rose, that tallness is found in me, that laziness is found in him. When we use words this way, we may act as if what we project outside ourselves can actually be found outside ourselves. Yet we know from the abstracting process that how we see or in other ways evaluate things comes from a transaction between what impacts on us and how we take in and interpret that impact.

Since we each evaluate at least somewhat differently, I may see as "red" what you may see as "pink". How will a "color-blind" person see the rose? How and who determines what "tall" 'means'? Have you ever felt "short" next to a much taller person and "tall" next to a much shorter person? What do we mean by "lazy"? Would everyone find the boy "lazy" in every situation?

So using GS, we might do best to avoid the 'is' of predication. We have other ways of phrasing our sentences. For example, we may say, "This rose looks red to me." We may say, "I feel tall now." We may say, "The child seems lazy to me." We thus acknowledge our nervous system evaluations as our own, not as existing outside of our nervous systems.

In writing this book, we have sought to avoid using the 'ises of identity and predication', except in examples demonstrating how they can be used and in quoting others. We do use the 'is not' of non-identity. We again discuss issues of rephrasing to avoid them in Chapter 13, on the extensional devices.

Non-Allness

The second and third aristotelian premises ("Anything is either A or not A" and "Something cannot be both A and not-A") may suggest an attitude of "allness", as if we can account for 'all' 'things' within our categories for describing them. We can contrast this with the non-aristotelian premise of "The map covers *not all* the territory," wherein we acknowledge that our maps (how we categorize and talk about things) cannot account for "all" non-verbal processes. Several important aspects of GS derive from these contrasting ways of evaluating.

Either/Or

These latter two aristotelian premises suggest an either/orness, encouraging us to evaluate as if every question can be answered by "yes *or* no". Yet, as we discussed in the last chapter, even facts don't necessarily fall neatly into these kinds of exact categories. Consider: Do you like where you live? Yes or no? Many people both like and dislike where they live to some degree. We often do best with "yes *and* no", "maybe", and other expressions of inclusiveness and in-between-ness.

Using "either/or" language, may make it easier to express what is called a two-valued orientation. When we use "both-and" language we're using what is called a MULTI-VALUED ORIENTATION. GS includes "either/or" when appropriate but goes beyond this to "both-and".

Thus we recognize that sometimes we find it useful to evaluate in either/or terms. If we're deciding what to do today, at some time we face the decision of taking one or another action: either to go out to the movies or to rent one to watch at home, for example. If we're deciding whether we like all apples, when we discover we don't like Granny Smiths, then we can say, no, we don't like all apples.

However, in reaching the point of these two-valued decisions, we do best by taking a multi-valued approach. This involves creating alternatives beyond either/or. So we don't start with only the choices, "go out or stay home to see a movie". We generate a multiplicity of choices: What could we do today? Yes, and what else? What else? etc., etc. From these "yes, and" possibilities, we stand a better chance of making a good choice.

If we see our only choices about apples as Golden Delicious or Red Delicious, we're cutting off possibilities. By noting many varieties of apples, we give ourselves the possibilities of not only rejecting Granny Smith, but enjoying McIntosh, Rome, and other varieties.

In our language we find many examples of limiting either/orness. We easily find dichotomies: good/bad, wonderful/terrible, tall/short, fat/thin, easy/hard, happy/sad, sick/well. We do best by recognizing the limits of an either/or orientation and increasing our vocabularies to reflect shades of in-between-ness.

For example, Susan finds that people benefit by listing as many 'emotions' as they can come up with, developing a long list over time. The list enables them to notice so much more about themselves, which allows them to notice differences and change. Similarly, Bruce finds that people benefit by being able to identify varieties of sensation, for example differentiating types of pain and differing sensations of comfort, etc., as a guide to treatment and noticing improvement.

We can benefit by recognizing our ability to develop multiple alternatives in any situation. When we develop the habit of asking, "And what else?" we learn to recognize that we rarely have to restrict ourselves to one or two choices.

Causation

Another aspect of two-valued versus multi-valued involves issues of causation. If we believe that we can neatly categorize things in either/or terms, we may look for 'the' cause of something. However, recognizing the complex, multidimensional character of our silent-level experiencing, we can recognize the futility of this search. How can we ever know '*the*' cause? We do better to look for *a* cause; to look for cause*s*.

As we suggested in Chapter 6, when we look for how things are functionally related (what serves as a function of what), we do best to look at multiple causes and effects. Any factors related to the interacting of organisms-as-wholes-in-their-environments, past, present, and anticipating the future, can influence what happens.

Rather than saying, "My boss caused my failure," we can consider what we and the others in our work environment, including our boss, bring to the situation under consideration. When we consider the multiple factors involved we have much greater power to remedy problems.

Rather than saying, "Blankets cause warmth," we can consider the various ways we can influence how warm we feel. Rather than "Antibiotics made me get better," we can consider the various ways we can influence our health.

Rather than "You made me angry," we can consider the multiple internal and external factors that influence what we do. We thus increase our chances of staying warm, healthy and content; we better prepare ourselves for new complex situations.

Labeling

In our discussion of the structural differential, we noted that the first verbal level involves naming and describing. When we're naming, or labeling, relatively simple 'objects' (such as apples), we run into relatively little trouble, as long as we recognize that what we *call* it isn't "it".

Even here, however, we can create confusion if our labels create inadequate categories relative to the territory. For example, we had the experience of asking someone what kind of apple she wanted. "A regular apple", she replied. Apparently, her experience with apples was limited to one kind, leading her not to differentiate among Granny Smith, Golden Delicious, Rome, etc., etc. Her definition for "apple" limited her observations. If all we're looking for when we want an "apple" is what we call Red Delicious, then we may overlook the others as apples and possibly miss out on some fine eating experiences.

Inaccurate and inadequate labeling (defining) can have much more serious consequences, however. We'll consider two examples here.

What we call "AIDS" was originally called "GRID", an acronym for Gay-Related Immune Deficiency. This label derived from early observations of cases of immune deficiency, which seemed only to involve gay men. As Randy Shilts noted in *And the Band Played On*, early in the "AIDS" epidemic (1982) when it was called "GRID" many scientists refused to acknowledge the probability or even the possibility of the phenomenon affecting mothers and their babies—after all, "...by its very name GRID was a homosexual disease, not a disease of babies or their mothers."[90] This inadequate labeling had tragic consequences in delaying recognition of the disease and research about its many manifestations. The criteria for recognizing AIDS tended to limit diagnosing women, which led to overlooking many cases in women until they neared death.

Wendell Johnson, an expert in speech difficulties, and his students, studied the disorder called stuttering.[91] As of 1946, they found no verified cases of Native American Indians who stuttered, except two who had been raised and/or educated among whites. They also found that Native American Indians had no word for stuttering. It seemed that every child was regarded as a satisfactory speaker, no matter how the child spoke. Hesitations and repetitions were accepted; tensions did not build up around these normal nonfluencies. From these observations, Johnson formulated the notion of "diagnosogenic" disorders. He coined this term to indicate the risks of diagnosis, or labeling someone as belonging in a certain category. He noted that diagnosing something sometimes creates that which was diagnosed.

How often do such "diagnoses" or labels as smart, dumb, clumsy, failure, success, anxious, musical, not artistic, etc., create disorders in how people function? We may say, "I am not artistic," leading us to avoid drawing and so not learn how well we can draw, and how to draw better. We may say, "I am a success," leading us to believe we don't have more to learn and so end up less successful when a new situation may require new learning. We may say, "I am an anxious person," and then avoid certain situations, preventing ourselves from learning how to overcome specific anxieties.

We do well to recognize these labels as higher-order abstractions, to avoid them and to refer back to the particulars in a particular situation. We do well to question what we 'mean' by various labels. Questions of 'meaning' bring us to issues of self-reflexiveness, as we continue our discussion of language structure in the next chapter.

Applications

1. Choose a dozen or more different 'objects' from around your home, office, yard, etc. Decide upon a category – for example 'green' things – and divide the objects into two groups, 'greens' and 'not-greens'. List the objects that you have placed in each group. Then pick another category and divide up the objects again, and again record your listing. You can do this any number of times over a period of time. Notice whether some objects seem easier or more difficult to fit into a particular category. If you do this application with other people, notice which objects others have placed in each category. Does everyone agree? Notice how, with each succeeding category, different objects may be classified into one group or opposing groups.

2. Consider the following statement of anthropologist Gregory Bateson. How can you connect this to our discussion of elementalism/non-elementalism and the organism-as-a-whole-in-environments? (See note for our views.)

> ...The unit of survival is *organism* plus *environment*. We are learning by bitter experience that the organism which destroys its environment destroys itself.[92]

3. Write, and then read, a one-page description about yourself using the ises of identity and predication. Now reword the description eliminating the ises of identity and predication, and then read the revised description. What differences do you find? How do you react to each description? How could these differences make a difference for you?

4. What is responsible for you reading this book at this moment? What else? Etc.

5. How do these experiments and questions help you to work on your personal concerns?

Chapter 11

Self-Reflexive Mapping

As humans, we are born with (and can escalate) a trait that other creatures rarely possess: the ability to think about our thinking. We are not only natural philosophers, we can philosophize about our philosophy, reason about our reasoning... We can, though we do not have to, observe and judge our own goals, desires, and purposes. We can examine, review, and change them. We can also see and reflect upon our changed ideas, emotions and doings. And we can change them. And change them again—and again!

Albert Ellis[93]

If we reflect upon our languages, we find that at best they must be considered only as maps. A word is not the object it represents; and languages exhibit also this peculiar self-reflexiveness, that we can analyze languages by linguistic means. This self-reflexiveness of languages introduces serious complexities, which can only be solved by the theory of multiordinality...The disregard of these complexities is tragically disastrous in daily life and science.

Alfred Korzybski[94]

The third non-aristotelian premise states a view of maps as self-reflexive. This reflects the notion that we can make maps of our maps; we can talk about our talking, 'think' about our 'thinking', react to our reactions. It also reflects the notion that our maps serve as pictures of our nervous systems as much as they serve as pictures of what we're mapping. In other words, we map our nervous systems along with anything else, so that whatever we say says something about ourselves as well as the topic we're talking about.

Thus, we question the common sense question, "What does that word 'mean'?" General-semantics uncommon sense suggests we use the more appropriate question, "What do *you* 'mean' when you use that word?" Because the word 'mean' may imply that 'meaning' exists apart from a 'meaning'-maker, we put it in quotes.

These aspects of self-reflexiveness lead to multiplicity in our abstracting and evaluating. Words involve multiple 'meanings' and 'meanings' change according to context, differently for each of us. We can call words 'meaningless' until we know the context in which they are used; hence the importance of the "What do you 'mean'?" question.

Multi-'Meaning'

In English, the 500 most common words have about 14,000 dictionary definitions. We refer to this as the MULTI-'MEANING' OF TERMS. How do we determine what is intended when a word is used? Can you know what "duck" 'means'? How about "run"? We need to take into account the context in which the word is used. Perhaps you've been asked by someone, "What does this word 'mean'?" You may reply, "Read the sentence to me." You are acknowledging that you need to know the "whole-word-in-its-environment" in order to attempt to answer the question.

Suppose you have the context and look up the word in a dictionary. What dictionary do you use? We looked up the first definition of "abandon" in three dictionaries. In *Webster's Seventh New Collegiate Dictionary* (1963) we find, "to give up with the intent of never again claiming a right or interest in". In *Webster's Ninth New Collegiate Dictionary* (1987) we find, "to give up to the control or influence of another person or agent". In *Chambers Compact Dictionary* (1969) we find, "to give up". What is the 'real' 'meaning'?

Comparing the two *Webster's* dictionaries points out an important aspect of dictionaries. In the 1963 edition, "a" is followed by "aardvark". In the 1987 edition, "a" is followed by "aah". Where did the "aah" come from? Dictionaries change over time, reflecting changes in usage, the coinage of new words, the acceptability of words, different editors, etc.

Dictionaries cannot tell you what a word 'means' right now or in the future. They can only give you past usages.

Our use of words represents usage at a certain point in time—the present, and usage by a particular person. Every time a word is used it has a somewhat different 'meaning', since a different nervous system is producing it at a different time than it's ever been used before.

People who interact with us get used to the question, "What do you 'mean'?" For we assume that we cannot know precisely what another person intends this time unless we have an answer to that question.

For example, Susan had a new client who said, "I'm narcissistic." Susan said, "What do you mean by narcissistic?" At first he reacted indignantly and somewhat angrily, replying, "*You* should know. *You're* the psychologist." When she explained that she knew what some books said about narcissism but was interested in what *he* 'meant' in thus describing himself, he started to understand the uniqueness of his evaluating (and the importance of getting specific).

We don't intend to suggest that you ask "What do you 'mean'?" for every word you hear; conversation would come to a quick halt. We are suggesting that you maintain an awareness of the multiple 'meanings' of words and that you check out your understanding when important misunderstandings may occur.

In sum, we can say that words don't 'mean' anything; rather, people make 'meanings' with the way they use words. We can react most appropriately when we recognize the 'meanings' of what we 'mean' when we talk about 'meaning'.

Multiordinality

We make maps of our maps. In this book, we are mapping our understanding of Korzybski's and others' maps about GS. GS represents a map of Korzybski's map of time-binding and the abstracting process, etc.

How does this self-reflexive mapping of maps relate to our language use? What happens when we talk about our talking?

To review, mapping our maps is represented on the structural differential by the different levels of abstraction. Thus, on one level we have the event, or presumed process, we're mapping. On the next level, we have our silent-level mapping, or 'perceptual' experiences, discussed in detail in Chapter 8. Moving to the verbal level, we have our descriptions of our silent-level mapping; then our inferences based on our descriptions; then our inferences based on our inferences (generalizations, theories, etc.). As we've noted, this process theoretically can go on unendingly.

Using GS, we note that some of our most important words can be assigned definite 'meanings' only when we can specify the level of abstraction at which they function. We include such words as 'mean', 'love', 'hate', 'fear', 'prejudice', 'fault', 'notion', 'true', 'false', 'yes', 'no', 'fact', 'difference', 'reality', 'cause', 'effect', 'abstraction', 'evaluate', 'question', etc. Just as we cannot know what "duck" 'means' apart from the context of a particular situation and user, so we cannot know what "love", etc., 'mean' apart from the context of the level of abstraction. We call this aspect of abstracting MULTIORDINALITY. We call such words MULTIORDINAL TERMS.

A rough test for a multiordinal term consists of checking whether it can be applied to itself. For example, do you love someone? Do you love loving them? Do you love loving love? Do you have a prejudice against prejudice? What 'facts' can we learn about 'facts'? What inferences can we make about inferences? What can we assume about assumptions? How can we question our questions?

We can say that love$_2$ about love$_1$ is not the same as love$_1$. "I hate you" represents a very different use of "hate" from the "hate" in "I would hate hating you."

So-called 'paradoxes' relate to multiordinality. You may have heard the 'paradox' about Epimenides, a Cretan who said, "All Cretans are liars." Was Epimenides telling the truth? It seems as if Epimenides is lying if he tells the truth; he is telling the truth if he lies. How can this happen? After all, Cretans are Cretans; lies are lies; truth is truth—aren't they?

Yes *and* no, depending on your orientation. Yes, we have a 'paradox' from an aristotelian perspective. No, we have no 'paradox' from a non-aristotelian perspective.

Using multiordinality (and multi-'meaning'), we find the seeming contradiction disappears. Finding contradiction assumes that 'lie' and 'truth' have universal 'meanings', regardless of level of abstraction. It implies that we can talk 'meaningfully' about 'all' of something. Yet we recognize that our processes of abstracting belie these possibilities.

Thus, finding 'paradox' assumes the possibility that Epimenides can speak of 'all' Cretans including himself and, by implication, of 'all' their statements including the present one. Yet, we recognize that Epimenides can only talk 'meaningfully' about the 'truth' or 'falsity' of lower-order specific statements that have already been made. If he doesn't specify the level of abstraction to which he refers, in this case a particular statement or set of statements made by an individual Cretan – if he doesn't say what a particular Cretan is 'lying' about – his statement qualifies as 'meaningless'.

It seems useful to recognize this. As Korzybski wrote, "...we gain an enormous economy of 'time' and effort, as we stop 'the hunting of the snark'...or for a one-valued general definition of a *m.o.* [multiordinal] term..."[95]

Many arguments occur because people act as if they know what they're talking about when they use words such as 'lies' and 'truth', when these words have not been adequately specified. Have you ever been present during an argument about whether someone is telling the truth or not, for example? People can debate about this back and forth, meaninglessly, unendingly. But until someone asks, "What do we mean by 'truth' and how do we know?", understanding and possibly agreement cannot be reached.

Much humor involves playing with the multiordinality of terms. Regarding 'truth' and 'lies', baseball legend Yogi Berra is reported to have said, "Half the lies they tell me aren't true."[96] Ah, but which half of the lies are they lying about? We enjoy such "Goldwynism's" as "I'll give you a definite maybe." Movie producer Sam Goldwyn may have been referring to one of his competitor's productions when he said, "Go see it and see for yourself why you shouldn't see it." He recommended his own movies thusly, "Our comedies are not to be laughed at."[97] What about these statements causes many people to laugh?

Reacting to Our Reactions

One way to characterize multiordinality as an aspect of self-reflexiveness involves our ability to react to our reactions, then react to those reactions, then react to...etc., etc.—and become aware of this process. Understanding—*and using*—multiordinality we can help ourselves understand and better deal with some of our most important behavior.

We can use an example of anxiety and calmness. We may label ourselves as "anxious" and focus on anxiety. We can feel anxious; then feel anxious about feeling anxious; then anxious about feeling anxious about feeling anxious. Each level of anxiety reinforces the one that came before, resulting in spiraling anxiety. We then feel confirmed in our label of "anxious."

We can feel calm; then feel calm about feeling calm; then calm about feeling calm about feeling calm. Each level of calm reinforces the one that came before, resulting in increasing calmness.

Now suppose you're feeling calm but notice that others around you are running around excitedly. Perhaps you start to wonder and question to yourself: "What's going on? What am I missing? Maybe we're in danger. How can I be feeling so calm when they're running around?" You can thus start to feel anxious about feeling calm. What will probably happen to your calm feelings?

Now suppose you're feeling anxious, and anxious about these feelings. Someone says to you, "You don't need to feel upset about feeling anxious. Just about everyone does sometimes. Nothing bad will happen because you feel anxious." So you start to feel calmer about feeling anxious. What will probably happen to your lower-level anxious feelings?

We can refer to these levels of evaluation/behavior as lower-order and higher-order. We use "lower-order" to refer to our initial behavior in a situation, e.g., anxiety$_1$. We use "higher-order" to refer to our reactions to our reactions, e.g., anxiety$_2$ about anxiety$_1$. We can maintain, intensify or reduce our lower-order behavior by what we do at higher orders.

These processes involve the kind of neuro-evaluational, neuro-linguistic feedback loop we've referred to before. Our higher-order evaluations lead to results that become part of the ongoing process from which we further abstract.

This applies to world situations as well as individual 'feelings'. During the depression in the 1930s, President Franklin

D. Roosevelt said, "We have nothing to fear but fear itself." By this statement, he apparently hoped to reverse people's fear evaluations and help initiate processes of positive change. We can start to change prejudice when we develop a prejudice against it. We can start to evaluate better when we start to evaluate how we evaluate.

R. D. Laing developed and described what he referred to as "knots", which demonstrate multiordinality in interpersonal relationships. An example follows.

JILL I'm upset you are upset

JACK I'm not upset

JILL I'm upset that you're not upset that I'm upset you're upset

JACK I'm upset that you're upset that I'm not upset that you're upset that I'm upset, when I'm not.[98]

Confused? How many levels of 'upset' do we find here? What kinds of expectations do Jill and Jack seem to have about reacting to 'upset'? How might they begin to stop this spiraling process? Let's consider the notion of self-fulfilling prophesies and return to "logical fate".

Open Systems

Multiordinality is involved in what we call self-fulfilling prophecies. For example, we have expectations, expectations about those, etc., which further influence our behavior. We've referred to possible instances of this. Jack and Jill seem involved in this process. In the story of the man and the trashmen, we wondered if the man's expectations about the trashmen, his behavior and the subsequent events, might lead him to expect more of the same, and so behave similarly again. We noted that expecting that we can't draw will lead to behavior which will subsequently reinforce those expectations. Labeling ourselves and others in a certain way leads us to create expectations about

behavior, which in turn makes that behavior more likely, rein-
forcing those expectations. In this way, we create what appear
as closed systems. As with the nine dot problem, we may seem
stuck in a box of our multiordinal evaluating.

When he was doing the nine dot problem at a GS discussion group, our friend Crispin Hesford recalled the following
story. He was working as a grounds keeper and over some
years, as instructed by his boss, he had accumulated a huge
pile of brush. Then his boss told him that the time had come
to get rid of it. He hired some people to pull apart and haul
away the intertwined sticks. A day of work resulted in barely
diminishing the pile of apparently hopelessly intertwined
twigs. He could not afford to continue the task in this way.

What to do? Crispin decided to study the situation. As
we've noted, silent-level observation can lead to creative solutions. As he looked and looked, he suddenly abstracted the
pile, not as individual sticks, but as one thing—a large piece
of cheese. How do you handle a piece of cheese? You slice
it. So he got to work on the "cheese", getting the job done
quickly by slicing it into pieces with a chain saw.

We have some concern about this solution, in that using
a chain saw in this way could be very dangerous and isn't
a course of action we advocate. We also can note that this
problem could have been avoided if certain assumptions had
been questioned earlier. What assumptions may have gone
into the instruction to accumulate such a huge pile of brush,
rather than clear it away more often?

However, with the situation as given, Crispin solved the
problem by recognizing that he could step out of his "box",
re-evaluate his assumptions and re-map his previous mappings
(action-plan) to create a new, more useful map. We consider
this a good example of creatical evaluating.

Using multiordinality can help us better understand the
power of "logical fate". Spiraling expectations and other as-

sumptions lead to "more of the same". If we want different results, we do well to to step out of the box to uncover and change these higher-order evaluations.

We've noted that a scientific attitude depends on questioning and revising assumptions. Progress in our understanding results when we develop an openness to ongoing evaluations of our evaluations. Systems which allow for this kind of openness can adapt more appropriately to new information.

We can better understand Korzybski's characterization of GS as a non-aristotelian system when we understand multiordinality and open systems. GS can be viewed as a meta-system (a system about systems), in that we can use GS to evaluate other systems. And from a self-reflexive GS perspective, we remain open to evaluating and revising even GS.

In the following chapters, we focus on specific ways you can develop openness to re-evaluating and revising those ways of evaluating that may impede your progress.

Applications

1. Find opportunities to ask yourself and others, "What do you 'mean'?" What reactions do you get? What surprises do you get about what people, including yourself, 'mean'?

2. Analyze the following 'paradox' noted by Korzybski:

> In a village there was only one barber, who shaved only those who did not shave themselves. The question arises whether the barber shaves himself or not. If we say 'yes,' then he did not shave himself; if we say 'no,' then he shaved himself. In daily life we deal all the time with such paradoxes, which if not clarified result only in bewilderment.[99]

Korzybski's resolution of this revolves around his assertion that "The term 'barber' *as a term*, since it omits the living human being, is a label for a fiction, because there is no such thing as a 'barber' without a living human being."[100]

3. Consider the following "knot":

> JILL You think I am stupid
> JACK I don't think you're stupid
> JILL I must be stupid to think you think I'm
> stupid if you don't: or you must be lying.
> I am stupid every way:
> to think I'm stupid, if I am stupid
> to think I'm stupid, if I'm not stupid
> to think you think I'm stupid, if you don't.[101]

Write down the use of multiordinal terms. List them in terms of orders of abstracting, referring to the structural differential.

4. How do these experiments and questions help you to work on your personal concerns?

Chapter 12

The Extensional Orientation

I admire especially a certain prophetess who lived beside a lake in northern New York State about the year 1820. She announced to her numerous followers that she possessed the power of walking on water, and that she proposed to do so at 11 o'clock on a certain morning. At the stated time, the faithful assembled in their thousands beside the lake. She spoke to them saying: "Are you all entirely persuaded that I can walk on water?" With one voice they replied: "We are." "In that case," she announced, "there is no need for me to do so." And they all went home much edified.

Bertrand Russell[102]

...if you can only learn how to 'think' in terms of 'facts' instead of definition, we will have achieved what we wanted to achieve. It's one of the most difficult things to do. It will take you a long 'time' to do that.

Alfred Korzybski [103]

A revealing experiment with words was suggested by Korzybski. Choose a short, simple phrase or statement and proceed to define each word in it. Similarly, define each word in each definition and continue with each new definition you make. You may do this alone or with a partner, and can write down your responses to follow your trail of definitions.

Before you become irritated enough to stop the experiment you may find that you have started to go around in circles. We did this experiment, starting with the book title, *A Soprano on Her Head*. Pursuing just the word "soprano", we can summarize Bruce's trail from "woman" to "person" to "human being" to "creature" to "living thing" to "not dead" to "living thing" to "not dead"...he rather quickly had reached his "oy" point of circling.

When you begin to do this you have reached the level of UNDEFINED TERMS. At this level, if pressed for a definition, even if we feel that we know what we 'mean' by such a term, we cannot express it in other words without speaking in circles. We have reached the silent, non-verbal, unspeakable level.

As we noted in Chapters 4 and 6, the general-semantics terms "structure," "relation" and "order" mutually define each other. Thus they represent undefined terms, referring to the silent level. Some people might resist this conclusion. For them, the 'meanings' of words are in other words and they emphasize finding the 'right' words, the 'correct' verbal definitions to make progress in communications, problem-solving, etc. Although realizing the usefulness of verbal definitions, we reject this emphasis. As we've noted, ultimately words in themselves don't 'mean' anything. Rather, people 'mean'. And what people 'mean' ultimately must go beyond words.

Intensional and Extensional 'Meanings'

Let's look at different types of definitions. If you ask us what we 'mean' by the word "horse", we might define the word for you in other words and give you a dictionary definition. For example, *Webster's Ninth New Collegiate Dictionary* defines "horse", among other ways, as "a large solid-hoofed herbivorous mammal domesticated by man since a prehistoric period and used as a beast of burden". Such a definition fits the word "horse" into a larger verbal category or classification with particular properties and qualities, an important aspect of aristotelian evaluating. In GS, we call this an INTENSIONAL DEFINITION.

If you ask us what we mean by the word "horse" besides the intensional definition above, we might take you to a race-track or farm and show you a number of individual examples of horses. In GS, we call this way of defining words by example an EXTENSIONAL DEFINITION. We can do this quite strictly by pointing to some non-verbal 'things' or events which we intend by the word. We can also do this with words and other symbols by listing examples, showing you illustrations and videos, etc., of whatever we are defining.

We consider this equivalent to operational definitions in scientific work. These describe "operations", that is, what someone needs to do to experience the individual referents, the particular 'things', that you refer to with your words. A recipe for brownies provides an example of an operational definition.

Note that the word "horse" refers to an entire class of individuals. With an extensional, or operational, definition we enumerate, point to or describe in detail at least some individual horses, or whatever we are defining.

In the **Applications** section of Chapter 9, we asked you to evaluate some statements as 'true', false, or indeterminate. One of the statements reads, "My friend will enjoy the sto-ries in this book." This statement predicts a future event. To qualify as "true" or "false", we need to make some observa-tions to test the prediction. Until we do this, its relation to 'facts' remains indeterminate.

However, before we can make any observations we need to know more about what the speaker 'means', or intends by these words. The 'meaning' of the statement also qualifies as indeterminate. We consider the statement 'meaningless' until we ask the speaker "What do you 'mean'?"

Even to stop here will not do. If we ask, "What do you 'mean'?" the speaker might say, "You know, my friend will be amused by the stories, she'll really like them," etc. In other words, we may be given intensional definitions. Before we can make any observations we need to know what the speaker 'means' extensionally. Operationally, we need to be told which person, how many stories and what behaviors we need to observe to determine whether the statement qualifies as truish, given those 'meanings'.

Extensional and intensional definitions exist on a continuum with each other. At one end we have non-verbal pointing to non-verbal 'things' and at the other end verbal definitions of fictional entities like unicorns. Both sorts of definitions seem useful to us. As we've noted, we value the creativity of allowing ourselves to imagine fictions. However, we have a preference for extensional or operational definitions, as they favor evaluating in terms of facts rather than mere verbalisms.

Intensional and Extensional Orientations

Expanding this distinction between intensional and extensional definitions leads us to talk about intensional and extensional orientations and behavior.

When we orient ourselves by verbal definitions, when we prefer preserving our maps (even maps without territories) to checking them out against 'facts', when we fail to become aware of our assumptions and inferences and to test them out when possible, when we identify different levels of abstracting, we behave intensionally.

When we orient ourselves towards facts, when we check our maps against possible territories, when we clarify and test our inferences and assumptions, when we don't identify different orders of abstracting, we behave extensionally.

Intensional and extensional orientations also exist on a continuum. We know of no one who exhibits a purely extensional orientation. Unfortunately, abundant examples of people near the other end of the continuum exist. Some of them are confined to institutions. Some of them speak, write books, appear on radio and television and run institutions. Most of us appear somewhere in between.

In many ways our neuro-evaluational, neuro-linguistic environments encourage an intensional orientation. Verbal facility in the conventional wisdom of the dominant group —what biologist C.H. Waddington called COWDUNG for short—may get confused with intelligence.[104]

Korzybski told of a gathering he attended with a number of highly-regarded scientists. Someone had an I.Q. test which people took as a kind of party-game. Korzybski related that those he regarded as the most gifted did the worst on the test. They considered the ambiguities of the questions and attempted to understand the structures behind the words with the result that they tended not to respond as quickly with the 'correct' answer.[105]

Emphasis on 'the' 'right' answer, on verbal definitions and labels, often gets rewarded in school and in life and may actually work against learning from experience. Nobel-prize winning physicist Richard Feynman related how his father, a uniform salesman, taught him a scientific attitude. His father would take him for walks in the woods in the Catskill Mountains during summer vacation. He related how one of the other kids said to him:

"See that bird? What kind of bird is that?"

I said, "I haven't the slightest idea what kind of bird it is."

He says, "It's a brown-throated thrush. Your father doesn't teach you anything!"

But it was the opposite. He had already taught me:

"See that bird?" he says. "It's a Spencer's warbler." (I knew he didn't know the real name.) "Well, in Italian, it's a Chutto Lapittida. In Portuguese, it's a Bom da Peida. In Chinese, it's a Chung-long-tah, and in Japanese, it's a Katano Tekeda. You can know the name of that bird in all the languages of the world, but when you're finished, you'll know absolutely nothing whatever about the bird. You'll only know about humans in different places, and what they call the bird. So let's look at the bird and see what it's doing—that's what counts."[106]

We have observed that some health professionals and their clients can easily get stuck in intensional efforts to answer "What 'is' it?" in relation to their problems. For example, people with low back pain are often labeled with a profusion of diagnostic labels, including low back strain, sciatica (pain down the leg), arthritis, etc., which may not have much extensional basis.

Consider the term "arthritis". People often get labeled with this because someone saw some indication of "wear and tear" on an x-ray. This, despite the fact that such changes have been observed as well in people without any back pain.

In Susan's work in psychology and Bruce's physical therapy work, we extensionally focus both ourselves and our clients away from diagnostic labels and towards looking and seeing what and how they're doing.

Bruce finds that clients with back, neck and other musculoskeletal problems, can be helped by a careful, extensional analysis of their 'posture' and 'movement' and the effect of these on their symptoms. Treatment involves making use of specific positions and movements as exercises to reduce and abolish symptoms and also helping clients learn better posture-movement habits. A large part of this involves helping clients to become more extensional regarding themselves and their problems.

As noted in Chapter 8, this can involve people learning to focus on "the means whereby", an extensional focus. It also can involve silent-level observation of how they function.

Susan has found that diagnostic labels can point people away from what they had best examine in their lives. For example, her client's label, "I am narcissistic," had led him to experience a sense of stuckness and an excuse for not changing. She prefers a process which focuses us on what can be changed in the present to create a more satisfactory present and future.

This involves looking for such factors as all or nothing, either/or, black or white evaluating; overgeneralizing; failing to recognize that the past and present are not the same; and other examples of neglecting GS premises. Intensional definitions play a large part in this. As Albert Ellis so cogently formulates in Rational Emotive Behavior Therapy, people tend to live by their "shoulds" rather than their experiences.[107]

Perfectionism plays a large part. Susan often finds people caught in what Wendell Johnson called **IFD DISEASE**: *I*dealization (intensionally-held ideals), which lead to *F*rustration, which lead to *D*emoralization (depression).[108] We'll be discussing such problematic, higher-order idealized abstractions as "success" and how to extensionalize goals in more detail in Chapter 13.

We hope that our health care professionals consistently act as Susan's gynecologist did, in having a kidney x-ray done before surgery. When she explained to a young friend that this was done to locate her kidneys, he reacted in horror: "Doesn't the doctor know?" She further explained that he knew what the books said about the location of kidneys; now he wanted to know exactly where these particular kidneys were located.

As can be seen in Figure 12-1, not only locations, but shapes of organs vary. These illustrations are based on laboratory specimens. Referring to these stomachs, Dr. Roger J. Williams wrote, "It is evident that some stomachs hold six or eight times as much as others. It is no wonder from this standpoint that our eating habits are not all alike."[109] Intensionally assuming a 'typical stomach' or anything else ignores the anatomical, physiological, psychological, etc., individuality of people. With an extensional attitude, we expect such variations among individuals.

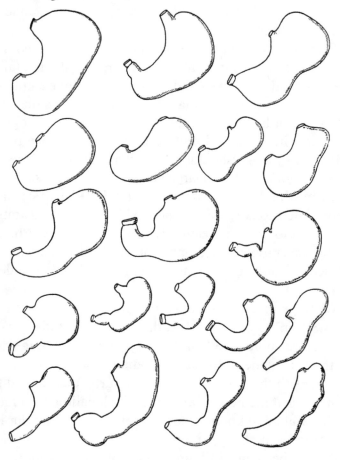

Figure 12-1 Stomach - Variations in Form[110]

These variations include the values people hold. We bought a house with a pool in the backyard. We decided to fill it in because we extensionally found that we prefer a garden to cement. Many people reacted with dismay or amazement: pool owners because they like their pools, evaluating intensionally that pools are good for everyone because they find it hard to accept that anyone would pay to undo what they had worked so hard to get done; others because they just believe intensionally, absent any experience with them, that pools are 'good'. We felt happy that the official rules (necessarily intensional) also indicate that pools increase the value of a house; our property taxes were reduced.

One more example involves the exhortation that people in the United States "Buy American". This may sound easy, even if you don't agree with it. Find "American products" and buy them. A newspaper pointed out the difficulties of following this intensional directive (although not using that term):

> Members of Congress have backed legislation to protect the U.S. auto industry. Business groups have aired "pro-American" ads...

> Some of the hysteria has backfired. Town leaders of Greece, N.Y. discovered that a Komatsu Ltd. excavating machine they had rejected was made in the United States and a John Deere Co. model they chose instead used an engine from Japan...

> For all their complaints about Japan, the Big Three often fail to note that Ford owns 24 percent of Mazda, GM owns 38 percent of Isuzu and Chrysler owns 11 percent of Mitsubishi Motors. Ford owns Jaguar outright, GM owns Lotus, and Chrysler owns Lamborghini.[111]

Thus, with the trend toward multinational production of goods, "Buy American" seems meaningless. If you want to buy "more American", you need to extensionally examine the production of each product and decide in each case what seems "most American".

An extensional orientation helps us to learn from experience. How can you learn how to learn this way? You have
already started. In the next chapter we will show you how
more explicitly.

Applications

1. Reread the first paragraph of this chapter. Perform the word
experiment if you have not already done so. How long does it take
you to reach your level of undefined terms?

2. Provide intensional and extensional (operational) definitions of
the following words: book, unicorn, happiness, democracy, structure, non-verbal, language, mango, spray-bottle. For extensional
definitions look for examples, things and events someone else could
observe; or describe in detail an example of what the word refers to.

3. Choose an activity like tying your shoelaces, tying your tie,
knitting, going some particular place, shifting gears while driving
a standard shift car or some other activity that you know how to do
well. Write a verbal description of it that could serve as directions
for someone who doesn't know how to do it. Give the description
to someone who doesn't know how to do the activity (or even
someone who does). How well can they follow the purely verbal
instructions compared to getting shown?

4. How do these experiments help you to work on your personal
concerns?

Chapter 13

Getting Extensional

The only man who behaves sensibly is my tailor; he takes my measure anew each time he sees me, whilst all the rest go on with their old measurements and expect them to fit me.

George Bernard Shaw[112]

...without changing the language itself, which is practically impossible, we can easily change the structure *of language to one free from false-to-fact implications. This change is feasible.*

Alfred Korzybski[113]

A cartoon shows a sleazy-looking real estate salesman cajoling a benighted-looking customer. They stand on a road leading up to a precipice at the end of which stands a single, tiny, ramshackle hut which appears just ready to collapse into the sea below. "Whaddaya mean, misleading advertising?" says the salesman. "Read it again, pal: cozy, quiet bungalow, exclusive neighborhood, balcony, great view, stone's throw from Pacific Ocean. Rent's reasonable, and you can move in right now. Whaddaya say? This offer won't last long."[114]

The salesman's words could intensionally fit ramshackle hut or desirable property. Extensionally they possess little 'meaning' until we actually view the particular house. And even this may not suffice. As Korzybski wrote:

> The dictionaries define 'house' as a 'building for human habitation or occupation', etc. Let us imagine that we buy a house; this buying is an extensional activity, usually with some consequences. If we orient ourselves by intension we are really buying a definition, although we may even inspect the house, which may appear desirable, etc. Then

suppose we move into the house with our furniture and the whole house collapses because termites have destroyed all the wood leaving only a shell, perhaps satisfying to the eye. Does the verbal definition of the house correspond to the extensional facts? Of course not. It becomes obvious then that by intension the term 'house' was over-defined, or over-limited, while by extension, or actual facts, it was hopelessly under-defined, as many important characteristics were left out. In no dictionary definition of a 'house' is the possibility of termites mentioned.[115]

Korzybski viewed most terms as OVER/UNDER DEFINED. "They are over-defined (over-limited) by intension, or verbal definition, because of our *belief* in the definition; and are hopelessly under-defined by extension or facts, when generalizations become merely hypothetical."[116]

We consider such *terms* indeterminate in extensional 'meaning' until we can specify them extensionally, in relation to non-verbal happenings. Such terms include so-called 'concrete' terms like 'horse', 'house', 'husband', 'wife', etc., as well as more general terms like 'peace', 'honor', 'freedom', 'love', 'hate', 'democracy', 'dictatorship', 'terrorism', 'law', 'order', 'capitalism', 'socialism', etc.

Going even further, we consider most *statements*, formulated using such terms, as indeterminate as well. We view most statements as functions, with the individual terms as variables which, as we have seen, can take on a range of 'meanings' depending on the context of listener, level of abstraction, etc.

Ken Johnson suggested a game based on this. Generate a list of some of the more general nouns. Write each word on a separate piece of paper. Then create various phrase templates such as "The _____ of _____" or "_____ against _____". Randomly choose pieces of paper and fill in the blanks with the words on them. You can end up with impressive catchphrases or book titles. Using the short list of words that we generated above we could create such titles as "The Dictatorship of Democracy", "Love against Capitalism", or "The Freedom of Honor".

As long as we realize the intensional nature of the game, we might even use it as a stimulus for creativity. Eventually, however, we need to bring such language down to earth by specifying variables such as 'dictatorship', 'democracy', 'love', 'capitalism', 'freedom', 'honor'. We need to critically evaluate such higher-order abstractions by getting extensional. Otherwise, we can fool ourselves because our randomly formed statements can sound 'profoundly meaningful' while conveying non-sense.

Delayed Evaluating

Here we return to the notion of delaying our immediate, automatic behavior so that we can fully engage our complex human nervous systems. We delineate two broad types of evaluating: SIGNAL and SYMBOL BEHAVIOR.

SIGNAL BEHAVIOR involves acting immediately and unconditionally based on past assumptions, expectations, etc., which may not fit the current situation. This undelayed, automatic evaluating is often triggered by unspecified higher-order abstractions. So we may get into an argument with someone about 'capitalism', based on our immediate assumptions about this general *word*.

SYMBOL BEHAVIOR involves delaying what we may do long enough to sufficiently investigate current conditions; making our actions condition*al*. Even conditions which might seem to call for immediate action benefit from at least a brief delay. As general-semantics scholar Harry Weinberg pointed out, "When a brick is falling from a building and you are under it, if someone yells, 'Look out!' there doesn't seem to be much time for evaluating the situation. Yet even here a quick glance might tell you which way to jump or you might jump under the brick."[117]

Extensional Devices

How can we delay our evaluations? How can we give more specific extensional 'meanings' to our words and statements in order to behave more sense-ably? The extensional devices give us means whereby we can extensionally relate our words and statements to life-'facts'.

The extensional devices consist of the following:

1. Indexing

2. Dating

3. Et cetera (etc.)

4. Quotes

5. Hyphens

We have used these as well as other extensional techniques and terminology throughout this book. Understanding them may seem simple. We consider this 'simplicity' deceptive. Verbal understanding is not enough; to benefit from them you need to *use* them. Using them explicitly in your speaking and writing at least some of the time, you can change the structure of your language and thus move towards more extensional evaluating and uncommon sense.

Indexing

The use of INDEXING comes from mathematics, where variables are given subscripts, for example x_1, x_2, x_3, etc. In our everyday language, the variables consist of the words we use. We consider any statement at least somewhat indeterminate or 'meaningless' in an extensional sense until we specify our terms using indexes.

A client had been referred to Bruce with a diagnosis of "degenerative disc disease". Bruce explained to him that he needed to get a history and perform an examination. The client appeared impatient and asked, "Doesn't the referral tell you what to do?" Bruce explained that he viewed every person, even with the 'same' diagnosis, as an individual, different from anyone else. "'Back'$_1$ is not 'back'$_2$", he said. Following this, the patient had no difficulty cooperating with the examination.

Our word categories lead us to focus on similarities rather than differences. Necessary and useful as this seems, however, no two individual people or things in any particular category are ever exactly the 'same'. No matter how similar they seem, differences remain.

Several years ago, we each bought a car, 'same' make, 'same' model, 'same' year. Besides differing in color, each car handled differently, with different engine sounds, different ride, and different 'feel' when shifting gears. 'Same' car?

Unless we index, we will tend to ignore such differences. Over-emphasizing similarities, we may identify one individual with another, and thereby with the verbal category that we have in our heads. By using indexes, we remind ourselves of the important differences between individual people, 'objects', events, etc. Almost automatically we can avoid identifying our categorical map with the individuals we're categorizing. This helps us to avoid identifying our words with our non-verbal experiences and the non-verbal territory. While maintaining links to other individuals in a category, indexing gives each individual its own separate sub-category.

How will we respond to individual humans if we continually index to remind ourselves that 'liberal'$_1$ is not 'liberal'$_2$, 'conservative'$_1$ is not 'conservative'$_2$, 'black'$_1$ is not 'black'$_2$, 'white'$_1$ is not 'white'$_2$, etc.? Perhaps we need not only less discrimination against individuals because of the categories we put them in, but also more discrimination between individuals by noticing how they differ.

We can also use indexes to help us to evaluate in terms of continuums or degrees. As we noted previously, the aristotelian language structure which we have inherited promotes either/or, two-valued formulating. For example, without indexes it seems easy to say, "You either feel pain, anxiety, etc., or you don't." Placing "pain" and "anxiety" on continuums, we can index them, say with 0 indicating no pain or anxiety and 10 indicating the maximum imaginable. In this way, we can more realistically note the degree nature of these variables. We can begin to notice and encourage degrees of improvement in ourselves and others rather than expect instantaneous, all-or-nothing results.

In addition, indexes prove useful in dealing with multiordinal terms. We can use indexes to talk about $anxiety_2$ about $anxiety_1$, $fear_2$ of $fear_1$, $enjoyment_2$ of $enjoyment_1$, $love_2$ of $love_1$, $hate_2$ of $hate_1$, etc. Indexing the level of abstraction can help us talk about such first-order and second-order reactions, deal with logical 'paradoxes', etc.

Korzybski advocated, as well, what he called "chain indexing", the multiordinal indexing of indexes to indicate the effects of environmental conditions, location, etc. Car_1 (with a full gas tank) will not work the same as car_1 (with an empty tank). We can note this as $car_{1,1}$ is not $car_{1,2}$.

The chain index or, as general-semantics writer Kenneth Keyes called it, the "where" index, helps us recognize "that any given person or thing may act differently when moved to a different place or placed in new circumstances."[118] Not only does back $patient_1$ not behave like back $patient_2$, but back $patient_1$ after walking for 30 minutes may have much less discomfort or no pain at all compared with back $patient_1$

after sitting slouched for 30 minutes. With chain indexing we can help ourselves and others to recognize the specific circumstances under which we feel pain, comfort, anxiety, enjoyment, etc. In this way we avoid acting as if every situation 'is' the same.

Dating

With indexing we have a way of indicating differences among individuals, matters of degree, levels of abstraction, and environmental conditions. We also need some way of indicating or indexing time-related differences.

As George Bernard Shaw's tailor realized, 'things' change over time. Not only does each customer differ from any other, but individual customers differ from themselves over time. The customer who, in 1991, weighed 198 pounds and had a 38 inch waist may, in 2010, weigh 220 pounds and have a 40 inch waist. A good tailor will take into account such changes over time and measure as necessary each time the customer calls.

Although we live in a process world of 'change thinging', we can intensionally evaluate and talk about it, ourselves included, as if time differences don't matter. To make our words and statements—and related evaluations—more extensional in regard to the time factor, we practice DATING, applying a date to the terms we use.

Dating helps us differentiate a particular individual at a given date from that individual at another date. It helps us to realize that no particular individual 'is' exactly the 'same' from moment to moment. You today are not you 10 years ago. In what ways have you changed? Some individuals, like the tailor, seem 'naturally' more extensional and thus more likely to take the time factor into account. Most of us need the reminding that dating our terms and statements gives us.

Et Cetera (Etc.)

Perhaps you have noted our frequent use of et cetera (etc.). The word comes from the Latin "and other things". We use it as an extensional device to indicate that we can never say all, that we can always say more about whatever we talk about. Since a map can never cover all the territory it represents, using "etc." indicates to ourselves and others that the last word has not been said.

Looking for and enumerating examples when we speak and write helps us get extensional about our higher-order abstractions. Using "etc." explicitly helps us to remember that, even after we've done this, we haven't said it all, thus promoting an et cetera attitude. When we have an et cetera or non-allness attitude, we ask ourselves: What might I have left out? What else? What other effects does this have, etc.?

Korzybski considered the use of "etc." so important and used it so often in his writings that he developed a special form of punctuation, utilizing a period (when combined with another punctuation mark) to stand for "etc."[119] For example, using this punctuation we would have written the last sentence in the last paragraph as "What other effects does this have,.?" The period before the question mark indicates "etc." We first noted Korzybski's use of this punctuation in the quotation of his at the beginning of Chapter 6, and note with [etc.] each subsequent time he uses it.

It seems useful to us to remember the "etc." whenever we see a period, to prevent us from having a "period and stop" attitude and encourage a "comma and more" attitude.

Quotes and Hyphens

We call indexes, dates and the et cetera "working devices" to indicate their usefulness in bringing the structure of our daily language more into accordance with life-facts. We also suggest the use of both quotes and hyphens as "safety devices" to use with elementalistic or metaphysical terminology.

We have used single quotes throughout this book to some-times flag words which have elementalistic or other false-to-fact implications. As we have already noted, we can elementalistically split with our language what is not split in the non-verbal world. For example, we can talk about the 'mind' and the 'body' as if some 'things' corresponding to these terms exist in the non-verbal world as separate entities. Yet as neuroscientist Gerald Edelman has pointed out, "...there has never been a solidly established demonstration of a mind without a body..."[120] Because of its metaphysical baggage we prefer eschewing the term 'mind' altogether. However, if we do choose to use this and other ques-tionable terms, we use them with quotes, when feasible. (When speaking, you can make quotes with your fingers or even—if just for yourself—your toes.) Using quotes we help alert ourselves to take care when we use such terms, as they may lead us astray if we use them uncritically.

We also use single quotes to mark off terms used meta-phorically or playfully.

Using hyphens, we connect terms that suggest separation of what we best understand as unified processes. The hyphen can help us remember what Korzybski called "the actual em-pirical complex inter-relatedness in this world."[121] In this way we can evaluate using non-elementalistic terms such as *space-time, psycho-biological, neuro-linguistic, neuro-evaluational* and *organism-as-a-whole-in-environments*.

Other Extensional Techniques

With the extensional devices, we have ways of observing and changing our own moment-to-moment language use—a good indicator of underlying orientation. Here we want to point out a number of other techniques that you can use to make your language and orientation more extensional.

Visualization

Drawings, diagrams, road maps, visual models, etc., generally work at lower orders of abstraction than verbal 'maps'.
Because of this, visualization often seems more direct than
words in showing possible non-verbal structure, relations,
etc. 'Thinking' in pictures has the potential to enhance your
language use and move your evaluating in a more extensional
direction. So we encourage you to practice drawing (however
crudely) what you see and 'mean'. But don't eschew words;
perhaps "a picture is worth a thousand words", but it takes
words to say that. And remember, your visual map is not the
territory either.

Non-Allness Terms

Using plurals rather than singular forms, and *a*, *an*, or
some rather than *the*, can keep us from looking for 'the cause'
and for single factors rather than cause*s* and multiple factors.
For example, as we've noted, Korzybski carefully called GS
a rather than *the* non-aristotelian system.

As problem-solvers we can restrict ourselves and our alternatives when we think in terms of "'the' 'best' way" rather
than "a better way" or "some better ways" to do something.
Talking about "'the' solution" rather than "a solution" or
"some solutions" contains a hidden assumption of absolutism
or allness, that this is the only way, period!

We need to take care when we use or imply *all* or *never*.
Unless we are dealing with pure mathematics, where by definition we *can* include all particulars that we are talking about,
we can never, as far as we know, say 'all' about anything.
And even generalizations, without explicitly saying 'all',
often imply hidden allness assumptions.

In a letter to the editor, we read that the reason "so many
people dislike rap music...is simple: rap is ugly."[122] 'All' rap

music? Has the writer heard all rap music? A limited *all*, such as "I find ugly all of the rap music that I've heard so far" would at least leave open the possibility of changing one's opinion with some new experience. Although rap isn't our favorite type of music, we believe this statement might come even closer to 'facts' if it was revised to "Some, but not all, rap seems ugly to me at this time."

Robert Anton Wilson suggested using *sombunall*—a shortened form of *some-but-not-all*—as a substitute sombunall of the time we use *all*.[123] So sombunall rap music may seem ugly. Sombunall politicians seem dishonest. Sombunall men seem sexist, etc. Perhaps you can find out what can happen when you begin to apply sombunall of the suggestions in this chapter and book sombunall of the time.

Qualifying and Quantifying

Qualifying phrases that specify the situation under which we are making a statement, and that acknowledge our role as evaluators, allow us to make quite definite statements extensionally. Such phrases as *as far as I know*, *under these circumstances* and *to me* help us to qualify and limit what might otherwise sound like over-generalizations. As far as we know, absolutistic ways of 'thinking' do not lead to sane ways of acting. Under these circumstances, if you wish to act more sanely, you would do well to use the extensional devices and techniques as much as possible. To us, using general semantics can lead to greater sanity.

Using phrases such as *up to a point* and *to a degree* helps nudge us away from either-or evaluating. They allow us to get beyond such questions as "Are you for me or against me?" Perhaps we can agree, to a degree, with someone whose views differ from ours.

Evaluating in terms of degrees, we realize that vitamin D helps build strong bones and that adding it to milk benefits our health, *up to a point*. We read about eight people diagnosed with vitamin D poisoning. They all drank one-half to three cups of milk daily from a Boston-area dairy. Samples of milk from the dairy showed some samples containing concentrations of the vitamin as high as 232,565 international units (the F.D.A. currently recommends 400).[124] Remembering non-additivity, we can see that more is not necessarily better.

Quantifying your language by getting answers, even rough ones, to questions such as *How many?* and *How much?* can help extensionalize what you say and do. Returning to the vitamin D poisonings, that particular article noted that the vitamin D was added to the milk by hand. Perhaps more attention to quantifying could have prevented problems.

One Step at a Time

We have already talked about the usefulness of 'thinking' in terms of *functions* and *variables*. Here we wish to emphasize the importance of remembering how functions and variables in your life can change in terms of *indefinitely small steps*. The part of mathematics called calculus deals with how functions change one small step at a time. You don't necessarily need to study calculus to get a 'feel' for the calculus that will help you to apply this notion in your everyday life.

Korzybski discussed getting a 'feel' for the calculus, more recently emphasized and expanded upon by GS scholar Milton Dawes. As Korzybski pointed out,

> ...the main importance of the calculus is in its central idea; namely, the study of a *continuous function* by following its history by *indefinitely small steps*, as the function *changes* when we give indefinitely small increments to the independent variable.[125]

Milton showed Bruce how to 'use the calculus' to improve his game of table tennis. He pointed out that where Bruce hit the ball was a function of many variables including, for example, how hard he hit it. By indexing the degrees of force, Bruce began to change in very small steps how hard he hit the ball and to note the effects. Observing the results of small changes—which sometimes have large, non-additive effects—he learned how to coach himself to improve his game as well as other aspects of his life.

Our friend Irene Ross Mayper marvelled at how useful she found this notion of the calculus and gave us the following example. She was working in an unfamiliar city and had walked to a restaurant for lunch. As she returned from lunch, she was faced with a big hill to climb (how much steeper hills can look when we need to go up, rather than down). Since she was having a problem with one knee, was wearing high heels, and the temperature had climbed to the high 80s, she faced this prospect with dread. Then she remembered the calculus. Taking each step as one small step at a time, she discovered that each small increment of placing one foot in front of the other did not seem to involve going up-hill. With each single step taken in this way, the 'hill' seemed to disappear. With an ease which amazed her, she found herself at the 'top', and 'feeling' high indeed.

English without "Ises" (E-Prime)

As we noted in Chapter 10, avoiding the "'is' of identity" (he is a politician) and the "'is' of predication" (the boy is lazy) helps us avoid identifying individuals with linguistic categories and qualities, with higher-order abstractions. We can more accurately say that *we classify him* as a politician or that the child *seems lazy to us*. In this way we make explicit our role in making these evaluations.

Bruce attended an event where a speaker gave an impassioned speech against abortion. "Abortion is murder and abortionists are murderers," he proclaimed. What kind of discussion do you think this might encourage, as opposed to a statement like the following, "Abortion seems like murder to me and I view abortionists as murderers." In the second case, the speaker acknowledges his responsibility in making this evaluation and he leaves open the possibility that he does not possess the absolute truth. Perhaps some agreement might be reached among those who disagree, but whose language reflects and encourages the kind of modesty that best suits fallible humans.

GS scholar D. David Bourland, Jr. formulated a subset of English, called **E-Prime**, which eliminates not only the "'ises' of identity and predication" but every form of the verb "to be".[126] Bourland advocated using E-Prime as a means of eliminating the undesirable "ises" from your vocabulary. Practicing E-Prime sombunall of the time can provide a valuable experience in discovering how use of the verb "to be" can influence your evaluating. However, we do not advocate completely abolishing the verb "to be" from usage all of the time. We agree with lexicographer and GS scholar Allen Walker Read who stated, "A plan to cut out every form of the verb to be would deny us the use of the progressive aspect and of the passive voice, and that would diminish the flexibility of English intolerably."[127]

English Minus Absolutisms (EMA)

As a broader alternative which may include some use of E-Prime, we espouse an approach to language use that Read formulated and labeled **EMA**, short for **English Minus Absolutisms**.

Read pointed out, "It is clear to many of us that we live in a process world, in which our judgments can only be probabilistic. Therefore we would do well to avoid finalistic, absolutistic terms. Can we ever find 'perfection' or 'certainty' or 'truth'? No! Then let us stop using such words in our formulations."[128]

Even when we remain aware that the 'meanings' of words are in us, certain words seem to carry an absolutistic baggage and we would do well to eschew them. According to Read, "When we find ourselves using the very common absolutisms such as *always, never, forever, eternity, pure, final, ultimate,* and so on, we could say to ourselves, was that term necessary? Could we frame our sentence in some other way?"[129]

Using the extensional devices and techniques, indeed the whole system of general semantics, changes the structure of our language towards EMA. By altering the structure of our language through EMA, we can gradually nudge ourselves, including our non-verbal behavior, in the direction of evaluating minus absolutisms.

Overcoming IFD Disease

In the last chapter (page 163), we noted problems associated with the perfectionism of identification-tinged idealism: what we referred to as IFD disease. For example, many people often set goals phrased as unspecified higher-order abstractions, such as "I want to be a success," or "I want to be happy." 'Success' and 'happy' can be viewed both as variables and as absolutisms. As phrased, we view these goals as unattainable; how would you know where to begin and how would you know when you got 'there'? As phrased, they function as terms which suggest opposites, in an either/or way. Either I'm a 'success' or a 'failure'; either I'm 'happy' or 'unhappy'.

These people can help themselves by applying the extensional devices and techniques to these terms (and goals). Thus, we can find less absolutistic terms to describe our wishes, eliminate the "'ises' of identity and predication", index and date 'success', acknowledge that individuals create their own definitions of goals and can re-evaluate them, etc.

Instead of "I want to be a 'success'" we might say, "I want to achieve such-and-such a result; I will follow these steps, starting on these dates, re-evaluating on this date," etc. With 'concrete', non-absolutistic goals, we can evaluate each step as we take it. At any point, then, we're less likely to evaluate ourselves as 'failures'; rather, we might say, "I'm not doing as well at step four as I'd like. What can I do differently?"

Extensionalizing leads to an emphasis on *doing* rather than on being; on *using* and *evaluating* what we know, not just collecting information. We find that this change in emphasis leads to much improvement in people's lives.

Questioning Questions

As we've noted, an important aspect of applying a scientific attitude involves asking clear answerable questions which can guide us to make useful observations. We talked about a child concerned about getting picked on. The child started out with the general question, "Why is everybody picking on me?"

We consider this an unanswerable question. Where and how would we find an answer to it? We need to know what the child intends by "everybody" and by "picking on". Further, even with these words defined, how would we determine the motivations of each child involved? This child was helped to come up with questions like, "Today, which children in my class called me names and poked me?" "Which children left me alone?" These questions lead to useful observations.

What can you observe about these questions in relation to an extensional orientation? They involve indexing, focusing on lower-order specifics and details. They involve dating, specifying when the behavior occurs. They involve non-allness, since we're no longer putting "everybody" into one category. Etc. In other words, useful questions ask: "Who?" "What?" "How?" "When?" "Where?" etc., designed to evoke concrete answers.

Similarly, a person might ask the unanswerable question, "Why am I not a success?" We find the question, "How can I be a 'success'?" slightly better, but still presenting problems. In order to begin to make some progress, we had better ask, "What do you mean by 'success'?" When answers to this question have provided some clarity, we can proceed with others. "What specific goals might help you achieve this?" "How will you go about attaining them?" "What first steps will you take?" "When?" Etc.

In applying extensional devices and techniques to your questions, you are internalizing GS, developing an extensional orientation. We suggest that you become more aware of the questions you ask yourself and others. You can experiment with phrasing them differently and discover what different kinds of answers you get.

We have phrased the questions in the **Applications** sections carefully. They could be rephrased, and many other questions asked about what we're presenting. What useful questions might you ask about GS? How might you answer them?

In the next chapter we explore further answers to the question: How can using an extensional orientation help us to create better lives and a better world?

Applications

1. Read a newspaper or magazine article, editorial, letter to the editor or advertisement. Pick out the over/under defined terms.

2. Next time you find yourself getting unduly upset, or at least exercised, when reading or hearing the news, discussing politics, etc.,

notice the extent to which you and others use over/under defined terms. Index and date these terms, and find out how this affects your ongoing reactions and discussion.

3. As Bob Pula suggested, date yourself! To do this, begin with the current date (for Bruce as he writes, August 23, 2010) and write the following sentence substituting your name:

> Bruce Kodish, August 23, 2010, is not Bruce Kodish, August 22, 2010.

> Bruce Kodish, August 22, 2010, is not Bruce Kodish, August 21, 2010.

Continue like this, going back one day at a time for one month, until you reach, in our example, July 23, 2010. Then go back from July 23, 2010, one week at a time for six months. Then go back by one month at a time for one year. Finally go back one year at a time to your date of birth, or conception. As you proceed, consider what changes have happened that show how you are not exactly the 'same' in all aspects from one date to another.

Consider the events (internal and external) that you associate with each date. To benefit from this, view it as an evaluating experiment, not a rote writing exercise.

Perhaps you become aware of particular changes related to current issues in your life. What happens when you focus on yourself as a process?

4. Choose one of the extensional devices or techniques that we have written about in this chapter. Practice using it for a day (or week). Write down examples of its use, or lack of use, that you become aware of. On another day (or week) choose another one to practice. Make special efforts to practice EMA. Etc. What difficulties do you encounter? What advantages do you gain?

5. Experiment using E-Prime. How does this go?

6. Consider 'the abortion issue'. How can using the extensional devices and techniques turn arguments into discussions? Use either already written material presenting each 'side' on this issue

or write a paragraph or two presenting each 'side'. Then revise the presentations using the extensional devices and techniques. What happens to the 'argument'? Practice this approach in conversations about this and other controversial topics.

7. How do these experiments and questions help you to work on your personal concerns?

Chapter 14

Time-Binding

If it is true that the unit of survival is the organism plus its environment, a sensitivity to the environment is the highest of survival skills and not a dangerous distraction. We must live in a wider space and a longer stretch of time. In thinking about survival, we must think of sustaining life across generations rather than accepting the short-term purposes of politicians and accountants.

Mary Catherine Bateson[130]

The origin of this work was a new functional definition of 'man', as formulated in 1921, based on an analysis of uniquely human potentialities; *namely, that each generation may begin where the former left off. This characteristic I called the 'time-binding' capacity...We* need not *blind ourselves with the old dogma that 'human nature cannot be changed', for we find that it* can be changed. *We must begin to realize our potentialities as humans, then we may approach the future with some hope.*

Alfred Korzybski[131]

We return to the issues of avoiding and getting out of messes and muddles. How can using GS—applying an extensional orientation—help us resolve individual, organizational and global problems?

Korzybski called one of his first papers *Time-Binding: The General Theory.*[132] He noted that, "This paper is a summary of a larger work on Human Engineering soon to be published." That work became *Science and Sanity.* (It was published nine years later; "soon" happens 'slowly' with such monumental work!) He considered calling his work "time-binding", so central a role did he see for this in his formulating.

Just as Korzybski's early paper served as a summary of his more complete work, so can our chapter on time-binding serve as a summary of this book. Understanding time-binding we note that, as humans, we do not only use chemical energy and 'space', as do plants and animals. We also, and most importantly, 'use' 'time', since we can use language and other symbols to consciously chart our past and present individual and cultural experiences and project into the future. Thus, in a way, 'all' that we've presented here represents time-binding.

Our higher brain functions involved in time-binding allow for consciousness of abstracting. This awareness enables us and others to formulate and write about: how we abstract; differentiating and not identifying levels of abstracting; transacting as organisms-as-wholes-in-environments; methods and results of science; mapping as the basis for knowledge; multidimensional complexities involved in functional relations; non-verbal awareness; language issues; etc.

How we use our time-binding capacities can have cataclysmic life-and-death consequences, as Korzybski noted in World War I. It can also have more subtle, long range consequences, such as how we handle education, population, environmental issues, etc.

Such issues seem increasingly important, as the accelerating rate of change results in spiraling technical changes, a deluge of information, ever-more-rapid global communication, etc. This leads many people to experience a sense of disorientation and insecurity; widespread conflict, confusion, anxiety, depression, etc., often are noted as signs of our times. Coping well with rapid change requires uncommon approaches.

Using GS involves uncommon methods for effectively using our time-binding capacities, as we particularly discussed in the last chapter. It also involves uncommon notions of responsibility in our individual and collective lives. As Weinberg said,

> Any form of thought, activity, custom, type of government, or theory is good to the degree that it fosters the development of effective time-binders; conversely, it is bad to the degree that it does not...Because the nervous systems of all men [people] are essentially the same, any custom which warps the functioning of the nervous system is bad, even if it is accepted by that society, for *in the long run* it will lead to its destruction.[133]

> Inherent, then, in our concept of the effective time-binder is an attitude, an ethical judgment, a moral precept as strong as any of the Ten Commandments...'So act as to make thyself a better time-binder; so act as to enable others to use their time-binding capacities more effectively.'[134]

Consciousness of abstracting enables us to take a long-term view; to ask the questions, "What kind of future do we want to project? How can we behave to encourage that future?" In considering these questions, we want to focus particularly on issues of taking responsibility, cooperating and communicating, three vital aspects of our time-binding capacities.

Taking Responsibility

Let's consider how consciousness of abstracting can help us understand human responsibility-taking at its best.

With such awareness we recognize that we each abstract differently. Effective time-binding involves taking responsibility for our own abstracting, and accepting inevitable individual differences in evaluating.

Your maps are not the territory, including your silent-level maps. In recognizing this, you can take responsibility for considering other people's maps. They may have useful ones.

Your maps are not all of the territory. You quite likely have left out important factors and can take responsibility for filling in gaps in your information.

Self-reflexively, you can make maps of your maps of your maps, etc. You can talk about your experiences and then talk about that talking, etc. You can take responsibility for evaluating any prior step and for figuring out how to re-evaluate what and how you are doing.

Also, your evaluations present a picture of your nervous system as well as a picture of what you're transacting with. In other words, your evaluations show the functioning of your nervous system. You can take responsibility for these evaluations as unique to you, avoiding a "know it all", superior attitude.

Able to differentiate among levels of abstracting, you can develop a 'fact-finding' orientation. We encourage you to join Korzybski, as we do, in following this approach. His longtime co-worker Marjorie Mercer Kendig wrote about him, "'I don't know, let's see!' was another pet saying of his, when faced with something new...he was his own best skeptic..."[135]

Consciousness of abstracting also helps us remember that every situation involves something new. You can take responsibility for delaying your immediate, automatic behavior to find out about the new. You can remain open and flexible when approaching each situation.

Through neuro-evaluational, neuro-linguistic feedback loops, we each contribute to the ongoing process world from which we abstract. Our behavior, our evaluations, form part of ongoing neuro-evaluational, neuro-linguistic environments; thus the importance of taking responsibility for those evaluations, non-verbal and verbal.

For the short-term and long-term, for ourselves and others, we do best by cooperating.

Cooperating

Most of us have heard the phrase, "survival of the fittest". Most of us fail to recognize that phrase as a variable; we can specify how it applies to animals and humans differently. Korzybski noted,

> The "survival of the fittest" for animals—for *space*-binders —is survival *in space*, which means fighting and other brutal forms of struggle; on the other hand, "survival of the fittest" for human beings *as such*—that is, for *time-binders* —is survival *in time*, which means intellectual or spiritual competition, struggle for excellence, for making the *best* survive. The-fittest-in-time—those who make the best survive—are those who do the most in producing values for all mankind including *posterity*. This is the scientific base for natural ethics...[136]

Note that Korzybski did not create an either/or position of competition versus cooperation; rather, he urges us to consider the kind of competition which contributes to human survival. Sports serve as an example of competition within cooperation; players compete to 'win', within a cooperative structure of game rules and guidelines.

Sports can also serve as an example of how that cooperation can break down. We read of violence at stadiums when some fans react to their teams 'losing'. We also read of violence when fans are celebrating a 'win'. Such failures to follow guidelines of 'good sportsmanship' within competitive situations seem to us good examples of very ineffective, short-sighted time-binding.

What kind of 'climate' (neuro-evaluational, neuro-linguistic environment) occurs when fans share 'good sportsmanship' rather than violence? What kind of 'climate' do you help create in your interactions? What 'climate' do you experience in your family, neighborhood, country? What difference does 'climate' make?

Juliet Nierenberg and Irene Ross Mayper highlight the importance of climate in their work on negotiating.

> Every negotiation has a climate. And more than any other single factor, this climate will affect the results of the negotiation. If you control the climate, you probably control the proceedings—for better or worse.
>
> Climate is fluid and changing and requires continual attention. It is the product of many things which can shift the mood ever so slightly or, in a moment, completely reverse it. The personalities, styles, feelings and attitudes of the people involved, the difficulty of the negotiation itself, the comfort or lack of it in the surroundings, the way people talk to each other—all affect the climate. What is perhaps less obvious, but more important, is the role of nonverbal communication.[137]

We can consider any interaction a "negotiation" and thus climate serves as an important factor for which we can take at least partial responsibility. 'Negative' climates diminish effective time-binding; 'positive' climates help us to use our nervous systems best, to foster growth, to realize our best potentialities.

You have probably had experiences where you and others functioned better, cooperated better, in climates of encouragement, laughter, etc., than in other climates. Susan found that work in her house went best when she created a positive climate among herself and her children. She discovered that they (and she) felt much more like cooperating to clean the house if she 'rewarded' them with a treat, such as going to the movies, before doing the work. This seemed much more effective in getting their cooperation and in all of them 'enjoying' the task than promising the treat for after the work was done.

Following the responsibility-taking guidelines we've discussed above will help you create positive climates, and hence the cooperation basic to human survival. We note this in efforts to improve the environment over the longer-term. Where we used to live, individuals cooperated to start and run a volunteer recycling center. County government became involved by providing bins and hauling the trash away. This led to increasing involvement of the county in curbside pickup of trash for recycling. Such efforts help encourage a more desirable future.

Taking responsibility, cooperating and communicating mutually define and relate to each other. What does GS imply for communicating?.

Communicating

Communicating well involves sensitivity to our environments, internal and external, taking into consideration the multidimensional complexities of our neuro-linguistic, neuro-evaluational environments. We can use GS to communicate in ways that encourage positive climates, help us achieve our goals and foster good relationships.

In discussing logical fate, we noted the importance of assumptions in whatever behavior follows. This seems particularly important in any communication. We come to any situation with a set of assumptions, premises, expectations, etc., which guides our subsequent communicating. Some particularly important ones include the following.

We sometimes expect consistency over time, not allowing for inevitable changes. This can take the form of criticisms which imply lack of change, such as "You always...", "You never...". (Notice the absolutisms here, so common in negative communicating.) On the other hand, unhappy with changes in any direction, you may want yourself and the other person to stay the same because you like the way things 'are'. You may complain, "How come you never...anymore?"

What effects can these expectations have? What climate is fostered? How might unhappiness with someone else's behavior get expressed better? How might greater happiness occur by accepting inevitable changes? Consider extensionalizing as you answer these questions.

Useful communicating involves recognizing individual differences in abstracting, as we discussed above. We can recognize that any behavior has multiple causes and engenders multiple complex effects. In trying to determine when something started, who started something, we each have our own perspectives. A classic example involves the wife who nags because her husband drinks; he drinks because she nags. Remembering that behaviors generally mutually define each other in complex ways, we can avoid such tangles.

Positive communicating involves respecting the individuality of each person. If we communicate on the basis of cherishing uniqueness—and don't we generally like and admire others for their uniqueness?—we can encourage improved uses of time-binding capacities.

This leads to expecting differences in evaluating. We frequently hear people say things like, "Everybody knows... ." "How could you be so stupid?" "What kind of person would do that?" These confrontational-sounding statements imply sameness in evaluating, phrased as unspecified absolutisms.

Phrasing something as a question does not make it a question. "How could you be so stupid?" seems to us a statement about the other person's supposed 'stupidity', not a seeking of information.

We communicate best when we seek to understand other people's assumptions and preferences. Failure to do this frequently shows up in how we 'help' others. Basing their actions on their own assumptions and preferences, people frequently offer what *they* would find helpful, rather than what *the other person* might find helpful. For example, perhaps person$_1$ prefers to be left alone when upset; person$_2$ prefers extra attention. When person$_2$ 'feels' upset, person$_1$ may stay away; when person$_1$ 'feels' upset, person$_2$ may pay extra attention. How much more helpful each would find the other if they communicated, accepted, and acted on these differences.

Positive communicating is fostered by non-verbal awareness. As you develop abilities to stay on the silent level, you can increase your sensitivity to yourself and others, get more in tune with ongoing changes, notice subtleties in behavior, etc.

You can non-verbally 'communicate' with other aspects of your environment as well. Appreciation of, and respect for, the world around you can increase as you focus on your sensations of that world. You can increase your aesthetic pleasures as you non-verbally experience sunsets, flowers, mountain views, theater, films, music, literature, etc.

As you learn to distinguish facts from inferences, you can increase your abilities to communicate. When you recognize higher-order abstractions as such, you may know when to seek more information. You may recognize the futility of upsetting yourself with such meaningless statements as, "If he loved me, he would..." or "If she was a real friend, she would...". You'll recognize 'love', 'real', 'friend' as variables defined differently by each person and differently in different situations.

A GS approach to communicating also involves a sensitivity to differences in language use. For example, when we lived in Baltimore, we met someone potentially interested in our professional services. However, we considered that he might not be interested in having his name on our mailing list, since he said he was "moving out west". To us, "out west" implies the west coast of the United States (a move we subsequently made). We discovered, however, that he was moving to western Maryland, not too far away then for our mailing list.

How did we find this out? We delayed immediately accepting our first interpretation; rather, we did some 'fact'-finding. Asking, "What do you mean?" to seek information leads to basing behavior on what is happening presently, with the particular people involved in the current situation.

We can summarize many of these aspects of useful communicating by returning to the use of extensional devices and techniques.

With "dating" we remember to ask, "When?" This helps us note and allow for changes over time, as well as make specific plans for the future.

With "indexing" we remember to ask, "Who?" "What?" "Where?" This helps us to note individual differences, to specify what is happening.

We avoid asking "Why?" "Why" questions generally can't be answered as stated: how do you know where to begin to find an answer, considering multidimensional causality? Answers usually involve higher-order abstractions. Also, asking "why?" often leads to blaming, as if someone must be wrong or at fault. While we advocate taking responsibility for our behavior, we discourage blaming others and ourselves. Blame creates negative environments, leading to negative time-binding.

Rather, we suggest asking "How did it happen?" This question generally results in 'concrete', lower-order-of-abstracting explanations, based on recent, particular behaviors. For example, in an argument people often say something like, "Why did you forget to stop at the store?" This generally comes across as a blaming accusation. You might more usefully ask, "How did it happen that you forgot? What was happening to distract you?" This can lead to useful problem-solving, to perhaps desired changes in behavior not likely to happen when the other person feels blamed.

Please note, however, that any question or statement can come across as blaming, depending on such non-verbal factors as tone of voice and emphasis. Can you imagine a tone of voice which would make "How did that happen?" sound like an accusation?

Using "etc." to remind ourselves that more can always be said, we can avoid "know-it-all" attitudes which can destroy efforts to communicate well. Keeping alert to what we may have left out we're more likely to respect the other people involved in any communication.

While quotes come more into play in written than spoken communication, we find it helpful to indicate quote marks with our fingers where we might use them when writing. Similarly, we can say "hyphen" where we might use a hyphen when writing.

In our examples in this chapter, we've noted some places where we communicate best by taking into account multidimensional factors. We can indicate this by using such non-allness forms as plurals and "a" instead of "the", and by using quantifiers and qualifiers. As we focus on one small step at a time and avoid absolutes, including the "ises" of identity and predication, we can become more and more clear in our communicating.

We are talking here about developing an *orientation* towards communicating which takes into account an extensional orientation, using general semantics.

Recognizing the multidimensional complexities of any communication helps us understand and accept that, as Kenneth Johnson said: "To communicate is to be misunderstood." Expecting lower-order misunderstandings can lead to higher-order understanding.

Personal Time-Binding

Part of time-binding involves each of us learning from ourselves, learning how to make the most of our individual experiences. We refer to this as personal time-binding. With personal time-binding, we recognize that we communicate with ourselves as well as others.

Most of us notice how frequently we talk to ourselves. We can use this internal chatter for worse and better. When we label ourselves "stupid" or similar negative higher-order abstractions, we create a negative time-binding environment. When we make perfectionistic demands on ourselves, unconditionally and absolutistically telling ourselves what we "should" do, as Albert Ellis emphasized throughout his writings,[138] we diminish our chances of fully realizing our potentialities. Instead, we can extensionalize our internal chatter, just as we extensionalize our talk with others. For example, we may use conditional "shoulds", such as, "If I want a cleaner environment, I should recycle whatever I can." "If I want good relationships, I should take responsibility for how I act."

We can not only take responsibility for our behavior, but take responsibility for treating ourselves well. You can use your time-binding capacities most effectively by cooperating with yourself, creating a positive internal climate.

Environmentalists use the slogan, "Think globally – act locally." How can we each act so that we "think of sustaining life across generations" as suggested by Mary Catherine Bateson; so that we allow for "survival *in time*" as suggested by Korzybski?

Applications

1. Ask yourself, and then others: What kind of future do you want? What kind of future would you like for the generation which follows you? What steps can you take to encourage these futures?

2. Practice saying, "I don't know," when asked about something 'new'. What happens inside and outside yourself when you do this?

3. Begin to notice the 'climate' of your interactions. What about your behavior contributes to better and worse climates?

4. What signs of cooperation do you note in your environments? In what areas of your life would you like to have more cooperation? How can you help this to happen?

5. Continue practicing using the extensional devices and other techniques.

6. Consider driving a car as an aspect of time-binding, with potentially disastrous consequences. When you're on the road, what evidence of poor time-binding can you note? How do drivers behave which suggests that they don't take responsibility for the effects of their behavior, that they compete without also cooperating, that they fail to communicate appropriately? How can you drive so that you allow for "survival *in time*", for "sustaining life across generations"?

Chapter 15

Et Cetera

Our experience supports Korzybski's belief that when we use general semantics, that is, get it into our nervous systems and apply it, not just talk about it, we get therapeutic effects. Thus, the title of Korzybski's book, *Science and Sanity*. Thus, the title of our book, *Drive Yourself Sane*.

Korzybski stressed GS as a preventive system:

Naturally in our work *prevention* is the main aim, and this can be accomplished only through education, and as far as the present is concerned, through *re*-education, and *re*-training of the human nervous system.[139]

We opine that doing the best for younger generations requires educating them in a non-aristotelian orientation, to prevent problems and help them develop and maintain 'sanity'. How about the rest of us, already so well-trained in the aristotelian orientation? In this book, we've suggested ways for you to begin re-educating and re-training your nervous systems by using the GS methodology.

How you approach this process can make a difference to your success. Korzybski suggested an "extensional theory of happiness".[140] This involves our expectations. When we have maximum expectations about any situation, that is, that things will turn out just as we want and anticipate, we will likely find the 'facts' of the situation less than we expected; we've set ourselves up for disappointment, frustration, depression, hostility, hopelessness, unsanity, etc. When we have minimum expectations about any situation, that is, we're prepared for not finding what we want, we will more likely find the 'facts' of the situation better than we expected; we've prepared ourselves for curiosity, change, excitement, happiness, hope, sanity, etc.

We suggest, therefore, an attitude of minimum expectations in regard to internalizing GS. We've been studying it for many years and are still learning. Any amount of any aspect of it that you learn can help you; allow yourself time for the process.

Also allow yourself to enjoy the process. You can develop an attitude of amusement about the sometimes extraordinary ways we all find to misevaluate. As you step back and delay your reactions, take time to laugh, to play with words, to smell the roses, apples, etc.

Beginners in any learning process often embrace new teachings with such fervor that they believe they must attempt to monitor their every action and word. While we appreciate any tendencies toward such fervor, we recommend that you treat yourself kindly in this regard. Remember that you're acquiring an orientation, not a straitjacket.

Beginners also often take upon themselves the task of enthusiastically spreading their new-found 'wisdom' to family and friends. We suggest that, for best long-term results, you temper this impulse. Remember that applying GS starts at home. You can expect to find sufficient examples of misevaluation in your own behavior to keep you amply busy. While we encourage you to share your increasing knowledge of GS with others, we suggest you avoid using it as a tool for bludgeoning other people to 'think' the way you do. They may come to you as they see positive changes.

We've stressed how we can use and learn from our experiences by understanding how we acquire those experiences and by applying a scientific attitude in our everyday lives, etc. Susan has described a fine example of this approach:

When my grandfather came to this country as a very young man and was faced with the need to earn a living, he looked around at what people did and decided he could and would like to paint houses. One day he went up to a painter working on a house and asked for a job. "Do you have experience?" the man asked. "Yes," replied Grandpa. So he was hired. As soon as he picked up the brush, the painter saw that he had never picked up a brush before and so fired him. When the next painter Grandpa approached asked him about experience and Grandpa said, "Yes," he was not lying. His insufficient experience led to his not keeping the second job either. But he didn't get fired until he had not only held the brush but also applied some paint. And so it went, with each job lasting a little longer and yielding more experience. Finally, my grandfather worked successfully as an independent house painter.[141]

As Korzybski said, "Don't talk. Do it."[142]

One advantage of having a general-semantics orientation involves giving up any attempt to say it all, since we know we can't. So we close this chapter wishing you pleasure in going on to other chapters of your life, with fun and advantage in learning from your experiences, as you develop uncommon sense, etc.

Applications

We suggest that you continue with your GS journal as a way of maintaining and extending your process of learning and application.

On Alfred Korzybski

Born in 1879 into the waning nobility of the Russian-occupied sector of partitioned Poland, Alfred Korzybski grew up on his family's estate, considered a model farm, and in Warsaw where his family owned an apartment building. As a child he quietly observed what went on around him, and learned from his engineer father to get the feel of the calculus and of the latest developments in mathematics and science. He also grew up with several languages (Polish, Russian, French and German), and later learned others; this gave him an early grasp of his later formulation, "the map is not the territory", "the word is not the thing".

Alfred Korzybski in his Chicago Office, 1944[143]

He trained as a chemical engineer. With no schooling in Latin and Greek, he found that regulations prevented him from formally pursuing interests in law, mathematics and physics. However, he read constantly in these subjects and in philosophy, history, literature, etc. He taught several subjects in a Polish school, traveled as a scholar through Europe, and worked to help educate the peasants employed on his family farm as a way of expressing his strong opposition to the injustices done them by Tsarist policies.

At the age of 35 when World War I started, he volunteered for service in a special cavalry unit of the Second Russian Army Intelligence Department reporting to the General Staff. He suffered several war injuries and deeply felt the suffering of others in the war. A later assignment took him to Canada as an artillery expert, and then to the United States, where he chose to stay. He learned English, developing a considerable command of this new language in a short time. He continued his efforts to help the Allies, first joining the French-Polish Army as a recruiter and then lecturing for the United States government, while he intensified his pondering about how the destruction and social collapse he'd seen could happen.

In 1919, he married Mira Edgerly, an American portrait painter. She recognized in him the characteristic concern for people and their plight which threaded through his early experiences and led him later to develop his work. As she said, "I had never met anyone with such a *capacity to care* for humanity-as-a-whole, as few men are capable of caring for one woman."[144] As he pondered questions raised by his experiences, he began to formulate his answer to what makes humans human, the notion of time-binding. He presented this theory in *Manhood of Humanity*, published in 1921. The mathematician Cassius J. Keyser, deeply impressed by this work, helped Korzybski edit the book.

Korzybski devoted the next twelve years to studying *how* humans 'bind time'. He studied the newest developments in mathematical foundations, mathematics, physics, anthropology, biology, colloidal chemistry, neurology, etc., focusing on how mathematicians and scientists evaluate when they do their work—representing time-binding at its best. He studied at St. Elizabeths Hospital, Washington, D.C., where psychiatrist William Alanson White, M.D., guided and collaborated with him as he investigated how psychiatric patients evaluate—representing time-binding at its worst. The evidence he gathered and the conclusions he drew in thus covering the gamut of human evaluating, provided the basis of his system.

He created the structural differential model and wrote and presented several papers on his work as it developed. In 1933, he published his major work, *Science and Sanity*, a record of his developing understandings and the formulation of his non-aristotelian system. Shortly before publishing his book he decided to call his practical theory of human evaluation "general semantics."

He then concerned himself with the question, "Does it work?" Did the application of his generalization of physico-mathematical methods actually benefit the evaluations and behavior of human beings? The remainder of his life was devoted to training students, evaluating the effects of training, and refining his system.

First in Chicago and later in Connecticut, before and after the founding of the Institute of General Semantics (IGS) in 1938, he worked days, evenings, weekends and holidays. He developed intense relationships with his students, "on whom he poured his energies hour after hour, as if it were of utmost importance for each individual to understand, to feel the weight of the world problems, the human values, he dealt with..."[145]

Under severe financial pressures, he continued his work and became a United States citizen in 1940. By the early forties his formulations had begun to penetrate into many fields. College courses were taught by his students; research into the efficacy of general semantics was done. These studies, as well as the experiences of psychiatrists using the methodology to help soldiers in World War II, supported its value. In 1942, his students in Chicago formed a separate organization, eventually known as the International Society for General Semantics (ISGS), to promote his work. They soon began publishing the quarterly journal *ETC.: A Review of General Semantics*.

In the late 1940s, Korzybski devoted much effort to studying, in historical perspective, dictatorships in general, and the evaluations of the people of the U.S.S.R. in particular. Consciousness of the mechanisms of evaluating remained a primary focus. In his later years, although slowed down by the fatigue engendered by his constant work and the results of his war injuries, he continued to teach and write to the end, which came suddenly on March 1, 1950, as a result of a mesenteric (lower abdominal) thrombosis and related complications.

Korzybski served as IGS Director during his lifetime. M. Kendig followed him as Director until 1965, followed by a number of distinguished leaders including Charlotte Schuchardt Read, Elwood Murray, Christopher Sheldon, Robert P. Pula, Jeffrey A. Mordkowitz, Steve Stockdale and, presently, Lance Strate. In 2004, the ISGS merged with the Institute which continues to publish *ETC.*, the *General Semantics Bulletin* (the Institute yearbook published since 1950), and the newsletter *Time-Bindings*. An Alfred Korzybski Memorial Dinner and Lecture is held annually, usually in conjunction with an educational colloquium. A number of other organizations around the world also continue with GS-related study groups and educational programs including the Australian General Semantics Society and the Forum on Contemporary Theory with its associated Balvant Parekh Centre for General Semantics and Other Human Sciences in Baroda (Vadodara), Gujarat, India.

While Korzybski found many indications that his methods of extensionalizing and developing consciousness of abstracting can improve our abilities to understand ourselves and others, he remained aware of "...the limitations of his work, of himself as an individual, and of all humans. His theory of time-binding laid the embracing foundations for the study and realization of the potentialities of humans..."[146]

In writing about the development of his work since his death, Charlotte Schuchardt Read wrote in 1988:

> Many of the principles [of general semantics] have indeed permeated our culture, whether or not people know that Korzybski and other pioneers have been their source. We are, so to say, "catching up" in many ways to the 1933 formulations...With the increasing world-wide awakening and groping for ways to deal with what is going on, a growing world population, and greater dangers, I see perhaps an even greater need than fifty years ago for what [his] formulations have to offer.[147]

In 2010, the need continues for what Korzybski began.

What Did Alfred Want?[*]

Overture

School was done. Vacation time had come. Fourteen-year-old Alfred Korzybski took the train from Warsaw. Young Alfred was traveling from his family's home there to spend the summer at Rudnik, their country estate located in the gubernia (government district) of Piotrkow about 100 miles to the southwest. Although this was school vacation, Alfred didn't expect to idle at Rudnik. He would have time, no doubt, for recreation but he also had plenty of work to look forward to and also, no doubt, what he ruefully referred to as "troubles." As he later described himself, "I was a trouble shooter since [the age of] five. At home, servants, peasants, whenever we had troubles: [I heard] 'Alfred, do it.' And Alfred had to do the dirty work."[148] When he arrived home that day, fourteen year old Alfred indeed had some "dirty work" to do:

> I came to the station and a man was with horses and cart...
> to take me home. The moment I arrived home here burst
> [in] a peasant, 'Master, master, save my wife'. What hap-
> pened? She just had a child. And she had a hemorrhage.
> She's bleeding white. I just came, a boy of fourteen—'save
> her'. I knew nothing about that part of it, so I asked my
> mother, 'What in hell can I do?' To mama I didn't say hell.
> I meant it probably, but I didn't say it. 'What shall I do?'
> And my mother gave me orders, put pillows under her
> fanny, and put cotton in her. ...And I remember my do-
> ing that, putting her fanny up, and filling her with cotton.

* Originally presented as a talk entitled "What Did Alfred Want: A Biographers's Notes on Korzybski's Life and Work" (based on Bruce's research for *Korzybski: A Biography*). Given at the General Semantics Symposium "Creating The Future: Conscious Time Binding for a Better Tomorrow," at Fordham University, Lincoln Center Campus, November 15-16, 2008 and published in *General Semantics Bulletin* 74/75 (2009).

Of course, not knowing what I am doing. I did the best I could— successfully. It stopped the hemorrhage somehow. Helping nature, but all the time, remember, what happens, they ran to the boss and my mother didn't want to be with them that way, so I had to do it."[149]

Korzybski remained a practical troubleshooter all his life—although the scope of the troubles he would deal with came to embrace larger issues and more people than those on his family's farm. Orson Welles once said, "There are never many—never enough of them—but there are men born into the world with a gaze fixed on the widest possible horizon, men who can see without strain beyond the most distant horizon into that unconquered country we call the future."[150] Alfred Korzybski belonged in this company—which includes, of course, women as well as men.

We've entitled this supplemental chapter "What Did Alfred Want?" With Bruce having spent over half a decade in the nearly singular pursuit of writing Korzybski's biography (with major assistance from Susan), it seems to us that the question "What did he want?" ("What did he fix his gaze on?", "What did he seek?") qualifies as just about the most important one a biographer can ask. Indeed, "What does he (or she) want?"seems to us the primary question in understanding anyone's life, including one's own. The psychologist William McDougall, whom Korzybski met and briefly corresponded with, put it this way:

The most fundamental fact about human life is that from moment to moment each one of us is constantly engaged in striving to bring about, to realize, to make actual, that which he conceives is possible and desires to achieve, whether it is only the securing of his next meal, the control of his temper, or the realization of a great ideal. Man is fundamentally a purposive, striving creature. He...longs for what is not."[151]

Korzybski also indicated the importance of this question. For instance, he taught that one of the keys to understanding an author was to get behind his words and to find out what he was trying to get across, what he wanted to accomplish in saying whatever he said.

We'd like to share with you some of what we've discovered as we've tried to answer the question, "What Did Alfred Want?" In Korzybski's case, he had his gaze fixed on something wide and far.

Time-Binding

By the time he wrote his first book, Korzybski had fixed his gaze upon perhaps the ultimate human horizon—the potential of the human race—summarized in the term "time-binding." Time-binding, for him, stood for the capacity which characterized the human class of life. As he presented it in his first book *Manhood of Humanity* (published in 1921), this capacity consists of the uniquely human ability to begin where another individual or generation has left off. Thus we can build on previous efforts in order to make 'progress'.

Formulated as a capacity or potential to progress, time-binding is not ethically neutral. Rather, time-binding, as Korzybski formulated it, implies a normative judgment on behavior. It depicts humans not only in strictly 'descriptive' terms, i.e., as beings with highly developed, symbol-using nervous systems who communicate with others. The definition also implies an 'ought'—a criterion of values—as well, and thus has strong ethical implications.[152] This value-laden aspect of time-binding (with related difficulties in determining what constitutes progress) opens up a formulational 'can of worms'.[153]

But despite whatever problems the formulation may pose, all (legitimately all) of Korzybski's subsequent work—which came to be called "general semantics"—involved his efforts to investigate and explain the mechanisms of time-binding. How did it work or not work? How could it be made to work better? It was his attempt to provide a foundation for a sci-

ence of humanity, "a science and art of human engineering...
of directing the energies and capacities of human beings to
the advancement of human weal." [154] He wanted to reduce the
amount of preventable stupidity in science and life. He wanted
to help as many people as possible to live up to their potential
as time-binders. For Korzybski, science and mathematics
provided some of the best examples he knew of time-binding
behavior. We could also learn by contrasting this best in behavior with the worst, exemplified by people with the most
serious psychiatric disturbances. For this reason, he spent
two years studying abnormal behavior in the mid-1920s, at
St. Elizabeths Hospital, the Federal Asylum for the Insane in
Washington, D.C.

He felt he could make a definite contribution by developing a teachable system that summarized the methodological
wisdom he had gleaned from his studies in mathematics, the
physico-mathematical sciences, psychiatry, and other fields.
He once said that just as you can bring a horse to water but
cannot make it drink, you can bring a boy to college but you
cannot make him 'think'. To increase the chance of doing that,
you needed at least a method, a set of time-binding standards
for human evaluation that could be taught—even to a child.
This is what he offered with his work.

Korzybski was already 40 years old when he wrote the first
draft of *Manhood of Humanity*. It seems clear that the notion of
time-binding and the scientific-ethical project that—over the
next 30 years—resulted from it, constituted the crystallization
of deeply held values that Korzybski had already developed
over his lifetime. In particular, Korzybski felt a strong sense
of gratitude for what he had received from others. Even the
peasants and servants on his parent's farm had—through their
labor—provided him with the gift of time that allowed him to
pursue his early studies. Having received much, he showed
an early tendency to give to others in return.

For example, as a young man returning to Poland at the turn of the 20th Century after a long sojourn in Italy, Alfred had the sudden sobering realization that his boyhood peasant playmate still could not read as an adult. Alfred soon started a school for the peasants on his family's property, a short-lived project that got him into trouble with the Tsarist government. (One of his father's last gifts to him before dying was to keep him from getting sent to Siberia for this 'crime'.) Korzybski demonstrated this kind of behavior his whole life. Seeming to go out of his way to help others was actually very much his way.

This attitude of appreciation for the time-binding gifts of others and the attendant desire to be of service to others characterized his life and seems to us essential for understanding why he did what he did. In addition, it provides the necessary 'fuel' for those of us who wish to become more conscious time-binders ourselves. We must study the past and develop a sense of gratitude, an ability to ongoingly acknowledge the time-binding gifts we have received from others—the quick and the dead. And we must ongoingly be aware that what we do, even from moment to moment, will be part of what the future inherits—our children and the children of others, their children, their children's children, et cetera. Will what we do now provide them with a blessing or a curse?

"I Am Selfish!"

We'd like to end with a story that Korzybski often told to his seminar students. This version, which he gave at his 1948-1949 Winter Intensive Seminar, explains in part the purpose behind what he did:

> ...Some friends gave a dinner for my wife and me, and they invited also an Oxford graduate,...very wealthy, educated, Oxford and so on. He was extremely British in what is definitely known—it is seldom believed in America but they believe in it—that's the British theory of selfishness. And he was nagging me all through the dinner—I had of course to tell them some development in [my work]; naturally they all

expected me to say something. Well, I did. He was nagging, interrupting, and I was trying to explain to him time-binding, how we are not like animals, every one for himself and all of that, but we are interdependent. We build upon the work of the dead, and we depend on the work of every one else in our civilization and so on. And I was telling how I worked to get my formulations, to deal with human messes all around.

Then he began to pick at me: 'why was I so 'altruistic', doing all this work for my fellow men?'—I don't know what not. 'Oh, this 'altruism' would not work, there is no sense in it, a selfish outlook is the only workable one', and so on and so on, picking at me with his theories about 'selfishness'. And ultimately I got annoyed with that petty criticism, that picking at me. I just shut him up—successfully. I said, 'You want me to be selfish? I am selfish! I work the way I work because I don't want to live in a world made by men like you!' That shut him up alright.

In a way—this is serious—remember there is no sense talking whether I am selfish or not, because that argument remains valid that I am say 'altruistic' because I eventually want a better world for me to live in. But you see the argument: 'selfish'-'unselfish' is actually useless. It is a good place for quarreling... [155]

Coda

To paraphrase a line from Joseph Conrad's *Heart of Darkness*, "Mr. Korzybski, he dead." For each one of you reading this, there are more important living questions than "What did Alfred want?"—for example the question: "What do I want?" We are bold enough to believe that—with the systematic toolkit contained in *Drive Yourself Sane*—an understanding of what drove Korzybski's life and work[**] might help you to answer your own present questions, to widen and deepen the horizon of your own gaze, so that what you want and what you achieve become truly worthy of yourself as a time-binder. We bid you adieu.

[**] In *Korzybski: A Biography*, Bruce has written the first comprehensive and book-length account of Korzybski's life, with never-before-told details of what he sought and achieved in the course of his extraordinary career.

Glossary

ABSTRACTING; ABSTRACTING PROCESS: how our nervous systems map or construct our non-verbal experiences from the process world inside and outside our skins and in turn map our experiences with words and other symbols; as far as we know provides our only way of gathering and representing information.

ARISTOTELIAN ORIENTATION: the pre-modern system of making sense of experiences and using language, systematized by Aristotle (384-322 B.C.) and his followers; still widely used today.

CONSCIOUSNESS OF ABSTRACTING: basic goal of general semantics; using our human ability to function with awareness of how we get information, symbolize it, and communicate it to others; improves how we function individually, in groups, and as cultures.

CONVERGING INFERENCES: multiple inferences about a situation which lead to a similar conclusion, or set of conclusions; increases the probable accuracy of those conclusions.

DATING: attaching dates to our evaluations; reminds us of changes occurring over time.

DELAYED EVALUATING: our potential ability to stop our immediate, automatic behavior long enough to sufficiently investigate the current situation before acting.

DESCRIPTIVE LEVEL: the first verbal level; involves statements of fact, wherein we describe most specifically our past and/or present experiences.

ELEMENTALISM: unconsciously dividing up what we don't find so divided in the non-verbal, process world; in doing so we thereby neglect important relationships, contexts, connections; elementalisic language use suggests false-to-fact, static, isolated structures.

ENGLISH MINUS ABSOLUTISMS (EMA): avoiding the use of absolutistic terms when we speak and write.

E-PRIME: a form of English which eliminates all uses of the verb "to be".

ET CETERA (ETC.): how we note that we cannot 'know' or say all about anything; how we note that our abstracting processes theoretically can go on unendingly.

EVALUATE, EVALUATION, EVALUATIONAL (SEMANTIC) TRANSACTION : the organism-as-a-whole-in-environment response of an individual in terms of the 'meanings' he or she gives to words, symbols and other events; includes verbal and non-verbal factors, i.e., sensing-thinking-feeling-moving-doing-etc.

EVENT (PROCESS) LEVEL: the inferred processes from which we construct our experiences.

EXTENSIONAL: related to non-verbal happenings and lower-order descriptions and statements of fact.

EXTENSIONAL DEFINITION: defining words and statements by lower-order descriptions and examples and references to non-verbal experiences.

EXTENSIONAL DEVICES: methods, including Indexing, Dating, Etc., Quotes and Hyphens, originated by Korzybski to help us develop an extensional orientation, relating our words and statements to life-facts.

EXTENSIONAL ORIENTATION: an attitude towards living which involves flexibly orienting ourselves primarily to non-verbal happenings and facts; includes the ability to use intensional approaches when appropriate.

FUNCTION: in its mathematical sense expresses how things are related; also refers to what something does, how it works or operates.

GENERAL PRINCIPLE OF UNCERTAINTY: all human evaluating involves uncertainty due to how our nervous systems work; acceptance of the absolute individuality of events on non-verbal levels, which results in all statements about them having, not certainty, but only varying degrees of probability; as thus formulated in general semantics, a generalization of the more restricted uncertainty principle as formulated in physics.

GENERAL SEMANTICS: a general theory of evaluation which takes into account the interrelations among: what is happening in ourselves and the world around us, how we get our information about those happenings, how we talk about such information, and how we behave; an up-to-date, scientifically-based applied epistemology.

HYPHENS: connecting false-to-fact elementalistic words with hyphens, to suggest how they refer to inseparable non-verbal events.

IDENTIFICATION: assuming that any two individuals or things, or a particular individual or thing at different times, are the 'same', i.e., identical in all respects; confusing levels of abstraction.

IFD DISEASE: Idealization gone awry (involving identification) leading to Frustration, leading to Demoralization (Depression); a result of an intensional orientation.

INDEXING: making our terms and statements as descriptive as possible by emphasizing individual differences as well as similarities.

INFERENCE LEVEL$_1$: second-order verbal statements, involving statements about statements; goes beyond descriptive level statements of fact.

INFERENCE LEVEL$_2$: third-order and higher levels of verbal abstracting; inferences about inferences; generalizations; statements about statements about statements, etc.

INTENSIONAL: related to higher-order verbal definitions.

INTENSIONAL DEFINITION: defining words and statements with other words; definition by higher-order verbal statements and categories.

INTENSIONAL ORIENTATION: living life primarily according to rigidified, higher-order definitions, without reference to lower-order experiences.

LOGICAL FATE: a model which highlights how assumptions and behavioral consequences are related; from assumptions, consequences follow; to change consequences, examine and change assumptions.

MAP COVERS NOT ALL THE TERRITORY: basic non-aristotelian premise that no abstraction, or map, can be a complete picture of the territory it represents; non-allness.

MAP IS NOT THE TERRITORY: basic non-aristotelian premise that our abstractions, or 'maps', such as our experiences, images and words, are not the 'territories' that our experiences, images and words represent; non-identity.

MAP IS SELF-REFLEXIVE: basic non-aristotelian premise that we can make maps of our maps, i.e., abstract from our abstractions on different levels (symbolizing our symbols, thinking about thinking, talking about talking, etc.); relatedly, our abstractions, or maps, reflect the functioning of the map-maker.

MAPPING PROCESS: an analogy used to indicate how our nervous systems abstract; i.e., acquire and represent information.

MULTI-'MEANING' OF TERMS: recognition that terms have multiple 'meanings' depending on user, context, etc.; terms not clear until user, context, etc., are specified.

MULTIORDINALITY: refers to the multi-leveled, self-reflexive structure of human nervous system abstracting/evaluating, including languaging; we can 'think' about our 'thinking', have 'feelings' about our 'feelings', 'react' to our 'reactions', etc.

MULTIORDINAL TERMS: a multiordinal ($m.o$) term with one dictionary 'meaning' gets assigned a different and definite 'meaning'-in-use according to the level of abstraction on which it gets used; thus an $m.o$ term can self-reflexively apply to 'itself' at a lower level of abstraction; an $m.o$ term has no definite 'meaning', constitutes a variable, until the context of level of abstraction is specified.

MULTI-VALUED ORIENTATION: an orientation which takes into account complex, multidimensional, non-verbal processes; taking an attitude of "both-and" rather than the "either/or" attitude of a two-valued orientation.

'NATURAL' (APPROPRIATE) ORDER OF ABSTRACTING: orienting ourselves to non-verbal experiences first, then first-order verbal descriptions, then higher-order verbal inferences, generalizations, etc.

NEURO-LINGUISTIC ENVIRONMENTS: language use and language structure (products of our nervous systems) provide environments which affect our own and others' ongoing behavior.

NEURO-LINGUISTIC FEEDBACK LOOP: aspect of the abstracting process whereby our language and related evaluations influence our ongoing abstracting; the spiral manner in which our subsequent evaluating is influenced by our prior evaluating.

NEURO-EVALUATIONAL ENVIRONMENTS: 'meanings', or evaluational factors (products of our nervous systems), both non-verbal and verbal, provide environments which affect our own and others' ongoing behavior; Neuro-Semantic Environments.

NON-ALLNESS: we cannot 'know' or say all about anything.

NON-ARISTOTELIAN ORIENTATION: a system which includes and goes beyond the aristotelian system, taking into account the process world of constant change, the functioning of our nervous systems, the complexities involved in determining facts, etc.; a system of evaluation based on modern science-at-a-given-date and consciousness of abstracting.

NON-ELEMENTALISM: recognizing and remedying elementalisms—i.e., posited false-to-fact, static, isolated structures—in our evaluating and language by acknowledging relationships and making them explicit; no object exists in absolute isolation; to be is to be related.

NON-IDENTITY: no two individuals (objects, events, reactions, etc.) are identical (absolutely the same in all aspects); a map (an abstraction) is not identical with its territory (what it represents).

NON-VERBAL (SILENT) LEVELS: our experiences which precede language use; silent-level abstracting; object level.

OBJECT LEVEL: the level of non-verbal abstracting at which we experience so-called 'objects' of 'perception' inside, outside and on our skins; includes 'things' and non-verbal 'thinking', 'emotions', 'intuition', etc.; silent level.

ORDER: *See* STRUCTURE, RELATIONS, ORDER

ORGANISM-AS-A-WHOLE-IN-ENVIRONMENTS: the non-elementalistic notion that an individual functions as a 'totality' within a given environment; sensing-thinking-feeling-moving-doing-environment form an inseparable whole.

OVER/UNDER DEFINED TERMS: terms which are over-defined (over-limited) by verbal definition, with these definitions believed in as fact, and under-defined by (lacking in) specifics or facts.

QUOTES: using single quotes around words which require evaluating with care, since they may suggest false-to-fact structures; for example, 'mind', 'thoughts', 'feelings'; quotes also may mark off terms used metaphorically or playfully.

RELATIONS: *See* STRUCTURE, RELATIONS, ORDER.

SCIENTIFIC ATTITUDE: in GS, recommended as an approach for living; involves uncovering assumptions, asking answerable questions, investigating/testing and making observations to answer these questions, accurately reporting observations, revising assumptions, etc.; not to be confused with scientific 'knowledge', etc., at a given date.

SELF-REFLEXIVENESS: we can make maps of our maps; we can evaluate our evaluations; our maps reflect the functioning of ourselves, the map-makers.

SIGNAL BEHAVIOR: immediate, unconditional, intensionally-oriented behavior; undelayed evaluating.

STRUCTURAL DIFFERENTIAL: a map (or model) which represents our experiencing process; a map of the abstracting process by which we can accumulate and transmit knowledge.

STRUCTURE AS ONLY CONTENT OF KNOWLEDGE: knowledge as structural similarity between our nervous-system-constructed mapping and what we presume to map, with maximum probability of predictability at a given date as the goal; if all human knowledge derives from and constitutes nervous system processes, these processes must involve such similarity of structure on various levels of the nervous system.

STRUCTURE, RELATIONS, ORDER: mutually-defining terms, with structure referring to a complex or pattern of relations which involve some order; these terms are used to indicate how we make maps of territories; undefined terms in general semantics.

SYMBOL BEHAVIOR: condition*al* behavior which engages our higher brain processes, enabling us to act extensionally; delayed evaluating.

TIME-BINDING: the potential for each generation to start where the last generation left off; the potential for individuals to learn from their own and other people's experiences; the potential to become aware of this ability; this allows for the formation of cultures and the ability to study cultures, etc.; based upon the characteristic human ability, involving language and other symbolism, to transmit information across time.

UNDEFINED TERMS: terms which refer to non-verbal, silent-level, unspeakable experiences, which cannot be defined verbally except by speaking in circles.

VARIABLE: a term which can take on a range of values; an indeterminate quantity (quality) until further specified; a function relates two or more variables so that the particular value of one (the dependent variable) depends on the specific value given to the other(s) (independent variable(s)).

VERBAL LEVELS: the levels of abstracting which involve language.

Notes

Epigraph

1. Holtzman, pp. 78, 79.

On Reading This Book

2. Korzybski, *Science and Sanity*, p. xxxvii. (All references to Fifth Edition)

Chapter 1: Introductions

3. "Epistemology as centered in *neuro-linguistic, neuro-semantic* [evaluational] issues. Korzybski built squarely on the neuroscience of his day and affirmed the fundamental importance of epistemology (the study of how we know what we *say* we know) as the *sine qua non* for any sound system upon which to organize our interactions with our children, students, friends, lovers, bosses, trees, animals, government—the 'universe'. Becoming conscious of abstracting constitutes *applied* epistemology: *general semantics*." Pula, *Preface*, p. xviii.

Chapter 2: Glass Doors and Unicorns

4. Hilgard, et al., p. 191.

5. Korzybski, *Collected Writings*, p. 60.

6. Modified from Korzybski's model with permission, *Collected Writings*, p. 129.

7. Dr. Philip Graven, a psychiatrist, suggested this term to Korzybski. See *Collected Writings*, p. 162.

Chapter 3: Uncommon Sense

8. Gregory, *Odd Perceptions*, p. 221.

9. Korzybski, *Collected Writings*, p. 547.

10. Ackerknecht, pp. 186-188. The author also discusses Pasteur's work, referred to later in the text.

11. In Carrol, (Ed.), p. 135.

12. Modified from Korzybski's diagram with permission, *Collected Writings*, p.375.

13. *Ibid.*, p. 46.

14. *Ibid.*, p. 75.

15. Johnson, W., p. 49.

16. Howe and Greenberg, (Eds.), p. 496.

17. Popper's *Conjectures and Refutations: The Growth of Scientific Knowledge.*

18. Unless otherwise noted, our references to Milton Dawes, Kenneth Johnson, Stuart Mayper, Robert Pula, Charlotte Schuchardt Read and Allen Walker Read are based on their lectures and on conversations with them.

19. Korzybski, *Science and Sanity*, p. 93.

20. Many people get stuck in solving this problem because of the assumptions they bring to it. A common assumption, abstracted from the apparent 'square' created by the dots, involves staying within this 'square'. When we recognize that we can go outside of the square, we can solve it this way:

Regarding a three-line solution: This may seem 'impossible' if we assume our lines have to go through the center of each dot. When we give up this assumption, we can solve it this way:

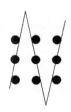

Chapter 4: Endless Complexities

21. Bruner, p. 22.

22. Korzybski, *Collected Writings*, p. 556.

23. Rossi, *The Psychobiology of Mind-Body Healing.*

24. Ibid., p. 16.

25. Ibid., pp. 11-12.

26. Russell, p. 104.

Chapter 5: The Process of Abstracting

27. Wilson, *Quantum Psychology*, p. 173.

28. Korzybski, *General Semantics Seminar 1937*, pp. 42-43.

29. Eddington, pp. ix-x.

30. Korzybski, *Collected Writings*, p.702. For more on change thinging see Pula 2000, p. 4.

31. Gregory (Ed.), *The Oxford Companion to the Mind*, p. 310.

32. These and other scientific developments are discussed in Korzybski's *Science and Sanity*.

33. Quoted in Korzybski, *Science and Sanity*, p. 368.

34. See Churchland; Edelman; and Gregory (Ed.), *The Oxford Companion to the Mind*, for further information about the nervous system.

35. Korzybski, *Science and Sanity*, pp. 379-380.

36. Modified from Korzybski with permission, *Collected Writings*, p. 566.

37. Roger Simon. *The Sun* (Baltimore). December 1, 1991, 1B; 2B.

Chapter 6: Mapping Structures

38. Kendig, p. 64.

39. Korzybski, *Science and Sanity*, p. 264.

40. See quotations in Korzybski, *Science and Sanity*, p. 85.

41. Hall, p. 16.

42. Ibid., p. 20.

43. Korzybski, *Science and Sanity*, p. 188.

44. Ibid., p. 632.

45. Johnson, W., p. 125.

46. Hardin, p. 58.

47. See Gleick's *Chaos: Making a New Science.*

48. Ehrlich & Ehrlich, p. 15.

49. Korzybski, *Collected Writings*, p. 704.

Chapter 7: The Structural Differential

50. Churchland, p. 482.

51. Korzybski, *Science and Sanity*, p. 448.

52. Modified from Korzybski's model with permission, *Collected Writings*, p. 129.

53. *Consumer Reports*, March 1992, p. 203.

54. *Consumer Reports*, May 1992, p. 347.

55. Korzybski, *Collected Writings*, p. 715.

56. Korzybski, *Science and Sanity*, p. 128.

57. Watts, pp. 34-35,

58. Lee, Part V, "On the Difference Between Words and Things".

59. Gregory, (Ed.), *The Oxford Companion to the Mind*, p. 514.

Chapter 8: Non-Verbal Awareness

60. Selver, p. 5.

61. Korzybski, *Science and Sanity*, p. 35.

62. Taken from Reps, p. 62.

63. Schuchardt (Read), p. 103.

64. Korzybski, *Manhood of Humanity*, pp. xlviii-xlix.

65. Read, C. S., "Exploring Relations Between Organismic Patterns and Korzybskian Formulations", p. 50.

66. Ibid.

67. Brooks, pp. 229-230. Information about sensory awareness can be obtained from the Sensory Awareness Foundation (http://www.sensory-awareness.org/).

68. See Alexander's *The Use of the Self* for his own description of his discoveries. Also see Jones for further discussion of the Alexander Technique.

69. Ristad, p. 79.

Chapter 9: Verbal Awareness

70. Paulos, pp. 37-38.

71. Korzybski, *Science and Sanity*, p. 415.

72. Korzybski, *Collected Writings*, pp. 685-686.

73. Lee, Part II, "Do You Know How to Make a Statement of Fact?"

74. LoLordo, Ann. *The Sun* (Baltimore). November 24, 1991, 6B.

75. Rosen, pp. 108-109.

76. Starr, p. 48.

77. Johnson, K. (Ed.).

78. (a) T: This statement reproduces the first sentence word-for-word.

(b) F: We have written nothing here about manufacturing computers.

(c) ?: We cannot evaluate this without more information about which friend, what is intended by "enjoy", etc.

(d) T: From our perspective, we view this as a fact, since we work hard in what we call our garden behind our house. From the reader's perspective this could be viewed as ?, since you didn't know if we were using a garden reference only as a metaphorical example, rather than a 'factual' description, or we may not be reporting accurately.

(e) F: Korzybski's premise directly contradicts this statement.

(f) ?: We need to know how Semmelweis functioned and what is intended by "good" and by "physician" to evaluate this.

(g) ?: We need to know more about which assumptions and what we intend by "trouble" to evaluate this. If we had phrased the statement, "Assumptions *can* get us into trouble", we would evaluate this as T.

(h) F: Information in the text contradicts this statement.

(i) F: If you trust Stuart Mayper's report of his observation, the text contradicts this statement. If you don't trust this report, evaluate this as ?.

(j) F: The text presents pure 'objectivity' as impossible to attain.

(k) ?: To evaluate this statement we need to know which people and under what circumstances.

Chapter 10: The Structure of Language

79. Hein, p. 17.

80. Korzybski, *Science and Sanity*, pp. 89-90.

81. Carrol (Ed.), pp. 210, 216. The accuracy of the Inuit (Eskimo) snow example has been challenged by anthropologist Laura Martin (Martin,

1986). On the basis of her work, Geoffrey Pullum has gone so far (irresponsibly in our opinion) as to call its use a "hoax" (Pullum, 1992). Martin's work has in turn been challenged by Stephen O. Murray (Murray, 1987). As we have noted, "No fact is simple."

82. Ibid., p. 243.

83. Ibid., p. 244.

84. See Johnson, W., pp. 6-10, and references to Aristotle throughout Korzybski, *Science and Sanity*.

85. See McNeill and Freiberger.

86. Korzybski, *Collected Writings*, p. 704.

87. See MacNeal.

88. Korzybski, *Science and Sanity*, p. 400.

89. Ibid.

90. Shilts, p. 124.

91. Johnson, W., pp. 439-466.

92. Bateson, G., p. 483. We prefer to talk of organism-environment, rather than organism +[plus] environment, to emphasize this as a non-elementalistic, *non-additive* relation. (See the sections **Functional Functioning** and **Non-Additivity** in Chapter 6.) Bateson's second sentence is consistent with our view, since it emphasizes non-elementalistic inseparability. In our opinion, Bateson didn't go far enough here in adopting a non-aristotelian orientation (or at least a non-aristotelian use of language); to talk of organism + environment may help perpetuate the very sort of behavior he decries.

Chapter 11: Self-Reflexive Mapping

93. Ellis, *How to Stubbornly Refuse to Make Yourself Miserable about Anything – Yes, Anything!*, pp. 14-15.

94. Korzybski, *Science and Sanity*, p. 58.

95. Ibid., p. 436.

96. Lederer, p. 134.

97. Ibid., pp. 129, 130, 131.

98. Laing, p. 21.

99. Korzybski, *Science and Sanity*, p. lxvi.

100. Ibid.

101. Laing, p. 22.

Chapter 12: The Extensional Orientation

102. Russell, pp. 110-111.

103. Qtd. in Mordkowitz 1985, p. 58.

104. Waddington, p. 16.

105. From an unpublished transcript of an interview with Korzybski: *Alfred Korzybski Biographical Material*, recorded by Kenneth Keyes, July 1947, pp. 45-46.

106. Feynman, pp. 13-14. Feynman overgeneralized here; what counts depends on what you are interested in. To an extensional student of language use, what humans in different places call the the bird may be what counts.

107. See **References** for a few of Ellis' many titles. *How to Stubbornly Refuse to Make Yourself Miserable about Anything – Yes, Anything!* serves as a good introduction. Information about these and other books and materials about Rational Emotive Behavior Therapy (REBT) and links to REBT-trained therapists can be obtained from the The REBT Network at http://www.rebtnetwork.org/.

108. Johnson, W., pp. 14-15.

109. Williams, p. 22.

110. Anson, p. 287.

111. Fatsis, Stefan & Ziegler, Bart. *The Sun* (Baltimore), February 2, 1992, 1D; 5D.

Chapter 13: Getting Extensional

112. As quoted in Johnson, K., *General Semantics: An Outline Survey*, p. 13.

113. Korzybski, *Science and Sanity*, p. lxiii.

114. Groening, p. 8.

115. Korzybski, *Science and Sanity*, p.lxv.

116. Ibid., lxiv.

117. Weinberg, p. 44.

118. Keyes, p. 141.

119. See Korzybski, *Science and Sanity*, pp. 15-16.

120. Edelman, p. 1.

121. Korzybski, *Collected Writings*, p. 709.

122. *The Sun* (Baltimore), 1/29/92.

123. Wilson, *The New Inquisition: Irrational Rationalism and the Citadel of Science*, p. 25.

124. K. A. Fackelmann 1992. "Vitamin D: Too Much of a Useful Thing." *Science News* 141 (18) May 2, p. 295.

125. Korzybski, *Science and Sanity*, p. 582.

126. See Bourland & Johnston (Eds.).

127. Read, A . W., "Changing Attitudes toward Korzybski's General Semantics", pp. 22-23.

128. Read, A.. W., "Language Revision by Deletion of Absolutisms", p.7.

129. Ibid., pp. 11-12.

Chapter 14: Time-Binding

130. Bateson, M. C., p. 234.

131. Korzybski, *Science and Sanity*, pp.xxxii & xxxv.

132. Korzybski, *Collected Writings*, pp. 55-90.

133. Weinberg, p. 158.

134. Ibid., p. 159.

135. Kendig, "A Memoir: Alfred Korzybski & His Work", pp. xxvi-xxvii. Kendig's essay provides a fine introduction to its subject.

136. Ibid., pp. 147-148.

137. Nierenberg & Ross, pp. 47-48.

138. See Note 107, Chapter 12.

Chapter 15: Et Cetera

139. Korzybski, *Science and Sanity*, p. lxxvii.

140. Korzybski, *General Semantics Seminar 1937*, p. 35.

141. Kodish, p. 142.

142. Korzybski, *Manhood of Humanity*, p. xxvi.

On Alfred Korzybski

143. Korzybski, *Collected Writings*, p. 482.
The sign on Korzybski's blackboard reads as follows:

> When a private at Randolph Field comes to a noncom with a complaint, he is handed a mourning-bordered card which says: "Your trials and tribulations have broken my heart. They are unique. I have never heard of anything like them before. As proof of my sympathy, I give you this card which entitles you to one hour of condolence. "

144. Ibid., p. 742. The material in this section is abstracted from the essay, "Alfred Habdank Skarbek Korzybski: A Biographical Sketch" by Charlotte Schuchardt Read and from *Korzybski: A Biography* by Bruce I. Kodish.

145. Ibid., p. 745.

146. Ibid., p. 748.

147. Read, Charlotte Schuchardt, "The Institute of General Semantics: A Brief Historical Survey," pp. 67-68.

What Did Alfred Want?

148. Korzybski 1947, p. 385.

149. Ibid., pp. 386–387.

150. Welles in Kodar and Silovic.

151. William McDougall, qtd. in Runkel, p. 32.

152. "On this inherently human level of interdependence time-binding leads inevitably to feelings of responsibility, duty toward others and the future, and therefore to some type of ethics, morals, and similar social and/or socio-cultural reactions." Korzybski in "What I Believe" (1949), *Alfred Korzybski Collected Writings*, pp. 646–647.

153. How do we determine whether the results of particular human efforts constitute 'progress' or not? Criminals in gangs seem to use their time-binding potential to cooperate and communicate with each other and learn from the experiences of other criminals and criminal gangs—sometimes for substantial benefits to themselves and fellow gang members while making things worse for the rest of us and, in the long run, for themselves as well. For further exploration of this issue, see GS scholar Jim French's "Editor's Essay 2004 – The Extensional Definition of Time-Binding," in *General Semantics Bulletin* 71: 8–9.

154. Korzybski 1921, p. 1.

155. This extended quote comes from the CD audio recording of Korzybski's 1948-1949 Winter Intensive Seminar (available for purchase from the Institute of General Semantics) combined with material (missing in the recording) from the unpublished transcript of the seminar.

Bibliography

Ackerknecht, Erwin H. 1982. *A Short History of Medicine, Revised Edition*. Baltimore, MD: The Johns Hopkins University Press.

Alexander, F. Matthias. 1932. *The Use of the Self*. New York: E. P. Dutton. Reprinted by Downey, CA: Centerline Press, 1984.

Anson, Barry J. 1950. *An Atlas of Human Anatomy*. Philadelphia: W.B. Saunders Company.

Bateson, Gregory. 1972. *Steps Toward an Ecology of Mind*. New York: Ballantine Books.

Bateson, Mary Catherine. 1989. *Composing a Life*. New York: The Atlantic Monthly Press.

Bois, J. Samuel. Edited by Gary David. 1966, 1996. *The Art of Awareness: A Handbook on Epistemics and General Semantics. Fourth Edition*. Santa Monica, CA: Continuum Press & Productions.

Bourland, D. David, Jr. & Johnston, Paul Dennithorne (Eds.). 1992. *To Be or Not: An E-Prime Anthology*. San Francisco, CA: The International Society for General Semantics.

Brooks, Charles V. W. 1974. *Sensory Awareness: The Rediscovery of Experiencing*. New York: The Viking Press.

Bruner, Jerome. 1993. "Life and Language in Autobiography". *General Semantics Bulletin* 57: 14-24.

Carrol, John B. (Ed.). 1956. *Language, Thought, and Reality: Selected Writings of Benjamin Lee Whorf*. Cambridge, MA: MIT Press.

Chambers Compact Dictionary. 1969. Edinburgh, Scotland: W. & R. Chambers Ltd.

Chase, Stuart. 1938. *The Tyranny of Words*. New York: Harcourt, Brace and Company.

Churchland, Patricia Smith. 1986. *Neurophilosophy: Toward a Unified Science of the Mind-Brain*. Cambridge, MA: MIT Press.

De Bono, Edward. 1969. *The Mechanism of Mind*. New York: Simon and Schuster.

Edelman, Gerald M. 1992. *Bright Air, Brilliant Fire: On the Matter of the Mind*. New York: Basic Books.

Eddington, A. S. 1928. *The Nature of the Physical World.* NY: The Macmillan Company.

Ehrlich, Paul R. & Ehrlich, Anne H. 1990. *The Population Explosion.* New York: Touchstone.

Ellis, Albert. 1975. *How to Live with a "Neurotic."* N. Hollywood, CA: Wilshire Book Company.

_____. 1988. *How to Stubbornly Refuse to Make Yourself Miserable about Anything – Yes, Anything!.* Secaucus, NJ: Lyle Stuart, Inc.

Ellis, Albert & Harper, Robert A. 1975. *A New Guide to Rational Living.* N. Hollywood, CA: Wilshire Book Company.

Feynman, Richard P. 1988. *What Do You Care What Other People Think?.* New York: W. W. Norton & Company, Inc.

French, Jim. 2004. "Editor's Essay 2004 – The Extensional Definition of Time-Binding" in *General Semantics Bulletin* 71: 8–9.

Gleick, James. 1987. *Chaos: Making a New Science.* New York: Penguin.

Gregory, Richard L. 1986. *Odd Perceptions.* New York: Methuen & Company.

_____. (Ed.). 1987. *The Oxford Companion to the Mind.* New York: Oxford University Press.

Groening, Matt. 1990. *The Big Book of Hell.* New York: Pantheon Book.

Hall, Stephen S. 1991. "Uncommon Landscapes: Maps in a New Age of Scientific Discovery". *The Sciences*, September/October: 16- 21.

Hardin, Garrett. 1985. *Filters Against Folly: How to Survive Despite Economists, Ecologists, and the Merely Eloquent.* New York: Viking Penguin Inc.

Hein, Piet. *Grooks.* 1966, 1969. Garden City, NY: Doubleday & Company Inc.

Hilgard, Ernest R., Atkinson, Rita L. & Atkinson, Richard C. 1979. *Introduction to Psychology, Seventh Edition.* New York: Harcourt Brace Jovanovich, Inc.

Holtzman, Harry. 1981. "Backing Up into the Future". *General Semantics Bulletin* 47: 76-80.

Howe, Irving & Greenberg, Eliezer (Eds.). 1968. *A Treasury of Yiddish Stories* (Abridged Edition). New York: Premier Books, Fawcett Library.

Johnson, Kenneth G. 1972. *General Semantics: An Outline Survey*. San Francisco, CA: International Society for General Semantics.

_____. (Ed.). 1991. *Thinking Creatically*. Englewood, NJ: Institute of General Semantics.

Johnson, Wendell. 1946. *People in Quandaries*. New York: Harper & Brothers.

Jones, Frank Pierce. 1976. *Body Awareness in Action: A Study of the Alexander Technique*. New York: Schocken Books.

Kendig, M. 1984. "Writings: Memoranda, Notes, Letters, Etc". *General Semantics Bulletin* 50: 58-91.

_____. 1950. "A Memoir: Alfred Korzybski & His Work" in *Manhood of Humanity* by Alfred Korzybski. Second Edition. Lakeville, CT: The International Non-Aristotelian Library Publishing Company, pp. xvii-xxxix.

Keyes, Kenneth S. 1963. Jr. *How to Develop Your Thinking Ability*. New York: McGraw-Hill Book Company, Inc.

Kodar, Oja and Vassili Silovic. 1995. *Orson Welles: The One Man Band*, on Disc 2 of *F for Fake: Criterion Collection*, special edition DVD. New York: Criterion, 2005.

Kodish, Susan Presby. 1989. "Resolving Tensions with General Semantics". *ETC.: A Review of General Semantics*, Summer, 46(2): 142- 146.

Korzybski, Alfred. 1921 *Manhood of Humanity: The Science and Art of Human Engineering*. E. P. Dutton and Company; Second Edition, Lakeville, CT: The International Non-aristotelian Library Publishing Company, 1950.

_____. 1933, 1994. *Science and Sanity: An Introduction to Non-aristotelian Systems and General Semantics*. Fifth Edition. Englewood, NJ: The International Non-Aristotelian Library Publishing Company.

_____. Edited by Homer J. Moore, Jr. 1937, 1964, 2002. *General Semantics Seminar 1937: Olivet College Lectures*. Third Edition. Brooklyn, NY: Institute of General Semantics.

_____. 1947. *Alfred Korzybski Biographical Material*. Recorded by Kenneth Keyes (July 1947). Transcribed by Roberta Rymer Keyes. Indexed by Robert P. Pula. Unpublished.

_____. 1990. *Alfred Korzybski Collected Writings: 1920-1950* (Collected and arranged by M. Kendig. Final editing and preparation for printing by Charlotte Schuchardt Read, with the assistance of Robert P. Pula.) Englewood, NJ: Institute of General Semantics.

Laing, R. D. 1972. *Knots*. New York: Vintage Books.

Lederer, Richard. 1989. *Anguished English: An Anthology of Accidental Assaults Upon Our Language*. New York: Dell Publishing.

Lee, Irving J. 1992. *Talking Sense* (video). Englewood, NJ: Institute of General Semantics.

MacNeal, Edward. 1994. *Mathsemantics: Making Numbers Talk Sense*. New York: Viking.

Martin, Laura. 1986. "Eskimo Words for Snow: A Case Study in the Genesis and Decay of an Anthropological Example". *American Anthropologist* 88 (June): 418-23.

McNeill, Daniel and Paul Freiberger. 1993. *Fuzzy Logic: The Discovery of a Revolutionary Computer Technology – And How It Is Changing Our World*. New York: Simon & Schuster.

Moore, Homer J. "Few Quandaries Here: An Analytical Review of Wendell Johnson's *People in Quandaries*". Unpublished Paper.

———. 2003. "Book Review of *People in Quandaries*". *General Semantics Bulletin* 69-70: 169-184.

Mordkowitz, Jeffrey A. 1985. "Listener's Guide to Alfred Korzybski's 1948-49 Intensive Seminar". *General Semantics Bulletin* 52: 51-76.

———. 2001. "A Note On Evaluational Reactions". *General Semantics Bulletin* 65-68: 87-88.

Murray, Stephen O. 1987. "Snowing Canonical Texts". *American Anthropologist* 89 (June): 443-44.

Nierenberg, Juliet & Ross, Irene S. 1985. *Women and the Art of Negotiating*. New York: Simon & Schuster, Inc.

Nelson-Haber, Molly. 2004. "Thomas E. Nelson: A Biography". *General Semantics Bulletin* 71: 7

Nelson, Thomas E. 2004. "On General Semantics and the Shaping of the Future". *General Semantics Bulletin* 71: 74-78.

Paulos, John Allen. 1988. *Innumeracy*. New York: Vintage Books.

Popper, Karl R. 1968. *Conjectures and Refutations: The Growth of Scientific Knowledge*. New York: Harper Torchbooks.

Pula, Robert P. 1994. "Preface to the Fifth Edition, 1993" in *Science and Sanity: An Introduction to Non-aristotelian Systems and General Semantics* by Alfred Korzybski. Fifth Edition. Englewood, NJ: The International Non-Aristotelian Library Publishing Company, pp. xiii-xxii.

——. 2000. *A General-Semantics Glossary: Pula's Guide for the Perplexed.* Concord, CA: International Society for General Semantics.

Pullum, Geoffrey K. 1992. *The Great Eskimo Vocabulary Hoax and Other Irreverent Essays on the Study of Language.* Chicago: University of Chicago Press.

Read, Allen Walker. 1984. "Changing Attitudes toward Korzybski's General Semantics". *General Semantics Bulletin* 51: 11-25.

_____. 1985. "Language Revision by Deletion of Absolutisms". *ETC.: A Review of General Semantics* 42 (1) Spring: 7-12.

Read, Charlotte Schuchardt. 1966. "Exploring Relations Between Organismic Patterns and Korzybskian Formulations". *General Semantics Bulletin* 32 & 33 (1965/1966): 47-52.

_____. 1989. "The Institute of General Semantics: A Brief Historical Survey". *General Semantics Bulletin* 54 (1988/89): 62-68.

Reps, Paul (Compiler). Undated. *Zen Flesh, Zen Bones.* Garden City, NY: Anchor Books, Doubleday Company, Inc.

Ristad, Eloise. 1982. *A Soprano on Her Head.* Moab, Utah: Real People Press.

Rosen, Sidney (Ed. & Commentator). 1982. *My Voice Will Go With You: The Teaching Tales of Milton H. Erickson.* New York: W. W. Norton & Company.

Rossi, Ernest Lawrence. 1986. *The Psychobiology of Mind-Body Healing.* New York: W. W. Norton & Company.

Runkel, Philip J. 2003. *People As Living Things: The Psychology of Perceptual Control.* Hayward, CA: Living Control Systems Publishing.

Russell, Bertrand. 1950. *Unpopular Essays.* New York: Simon and Schuster.

Schuchardt (Read), Charlotte. 1952. "Some Aspects of Behavior: Comments on Several Physiological Approaches". *General Semantics Bulletin,* 8 & 9 (Winter-Spring): 100-107.

Selver, Charlotte. 1957. "Sensory Awareness and Total Functioning". *General Semantics Bulletin* 20 & 21: 5-16.

Shilts, Randy. 1987. *And the Band Played On: Politics, People and the AIDS Epidemic.* New York: St. Martin's Press.

Starr, Deborah A . 1992. "Work in Progress". *Horticulture,* April :46-50.

Waddington, C. H. 1977. *Tools for Thought: How to Understand and Apply the Latest Scientific Techniques of Problem Solving.* New York: Basic Books, Inc.

Watts, Alan. 1971. *Does it Matter? Essays on Man's Relation to Material-ity.* New York: Vintage Books.

Webster's Ninth New Collegiate Dictionary. 1987. Springfield, MA: Mer-riam- Webster Inc., Publishers.

Webster's Seventh New Collegiate Dictionary. 1963. Springfield, MA: G. & C. Merriam Company, Publishers.

Weinberg, Harry L. 1959, 1973. *Levels of Knowing and Existence.* Second Edition. Lakeville, CT: Institute of General Semantics.

Williams, Roger J. 1956. *Biochemical Individuality: The Basis for the Genotrophic Concept.* Austin: The University of Texas Press.

Wilson, Robert Anton. 1986. *The New Inquisition: Irrational Rationalism and the Citadel of Science.* Phoenix, AZ: Falcon Press.

_____. 1990. *Quantum Psychology.* Phoenix, AZ: New Falcon Publica-tions.

Index

Abortion 179-180, 184

Abstracting 63, 67-69, 70, 72, 90-94, 97, 98, 112, 124, 132, 135, 149, 160

    consciousness of 63, 72, 89, 94, 96, 104, 114, 187-189

    'natural' order of 98, 109

    process of 63, 92-94, 97

Action potential 66, 67

Advertising 93

Aesthetic(s) 103, 194

Afferent 65

AIDS 142-143

Alexander, F. M. 108

Alexander Technique 108-109

Allow(ing) 107, 110

Alternatives, multiple 140

Altruism 211

Anatomy 75

Animals 27, 94

Answers 122

Anxiety 152-153

Arguments 151

Aristotelian orientation 130-132, 133, 134

    system 38

Aristotle 130

Art of Awareness 47

Assumptions 32-43, 70-71, 109-110, 192, 193

Asymmetrical relations 75-76

Australian General Semantics Society 205

Attitudes 33, 34, 102, 196

Back Pain 171, 172-173

Bandler 49

Barber 'paradox' 155

Bateson, Gregory 144, 223

Bateson, Mary Catherine 197

Behavior 33, 34, 38

    signal 169-170

    symbol 169-170

Beliefs 40

Benefit 38

Benefits 18

Berra, Yogi 151

Black swan 42

Black 171

Blaming 195-196

Body 46, 175

Bois, J. Samuel 47

Bourland, Jr., D. David 180

Brain 38, 50, 64-67, 97

Buy American 165

Calculus 178-179, 202

Calmness 152

Cannon, Walter 52

Carmichael, R. D. 62

Categories 125, 142, 143, 144, 171

Causation 141-142

Causes 83

Certainty 115-116

Change 54, 56, 60-61, 173, 178, 192

Chaos theory 84

Chase, Stuart 18

Chemistry-binders 27

Chudnovsky, David & Gregory 77

Circularity of human knowledge 94

Climate 190-192

Common sense 30-33, 37, 43

Communicate 50, 51

Communicating 192-196

Communications network 66

Competition-cooperation 190

Concepts 97

Conclusions 34, 35, 36, 42, 114

Conditional 169, 197

Confusion 187

Conrad, Joseph 211

Consequences 33, 34, 35, 36, 81-82, 83, 136, 142-143, 167, 187

Conservative 171

Contemplation 102-105

Context 147

Converging inferences 117-119, 125

Copy 94

Creatical 125, 155

Creativity 103, 125, 160, 169 See also Lateral thinking

Culture(s) 55

Current knowledge 24, 132

Dating 170, 173, 182, 195

Dawes, Milton 178-179

de Bono, Edward 38, 39

Definition 120, 142, 149, 157-159, 167-168

  dictionary 147, 158

  extensional 160

  intensional 160

  operational 159

  verbal 158

Delayed evaluating 64, 169-170

Demoralization 163

Depression 163, 187

Describe 25

Descriptive level 25, 26, 92

Diagnostic labels 142-143, 162-163

Differences 55, 137

Differentiations 129

Disappointment 95

Distinctions 129

Dogmatism 55

Driving 198

Duck-rabbit 70

Eddington, Arthur 60

Edelman, Gerald 175

Edgerly (Korzybska), Mira 203

Effect 83

Efferent 65

Ehrlich, Paul & Anne 85

Einstein 37, 62

Either/or 130, 139–141

Electro-chemical 66

Electron 60

Elementalism 135–136, 175

Ellis, Albert 14-15, 163, 197

Emotions 46, 83

Encyclopedia Britannica 76

English 130

English Minus Absolutisms (EMA) 180–181

Environment 47, 48, 49, 86, 135, 141, 144, 190, 197

  external 52-56, 192

  internal 50-52, 192

Epimenides 150-151

Epistemology 19, 218

E-Prime 179-180

Erickson, Milton 119, 124

Et cetera (etc.) 25, 26, 93, 170, 196

ETC.: A Review of General Semantics 18, 204, 205

Ethics 188

Euclidian system 37

Evaluate 19, 20, 23

Evaluation 46-47, 96, 170

Evaluational transactions 46-47, 49, 56, 87, See Semantic reactions

Event (process) level 24, 26, 90

Expectations 49, 50, 52, 57, 70, 85, 109, 192, 199-200

Experiences 19, 24, 27, 118-119, 189

Experiment 35-36, 109, 157

Exponential growth 85

Extensional
    behavior 98
    definition 159
    devices 99, 170, 175, 195-196
    orientations 98, 160

Extraterrestrial spacecraft 97

Fact(s) 25, 56, 114-116

Fact-finding orientation 189

Fact-inference continuum 116

Failure 181

False 122

Falsify 42-43

Fear 153

Feelings 46

Feynman, Richard 161

Flexibility 110

Friend 194

Frustration 163

Function(s) 80-83, 178

Future 27, 115, 188, 197

Fuzzy logic 133

General Semantics Bulletin 18, 19, 205

General semantics 17, 22-24

Generalizations 25, 32

German Shepherd 71-72

Gindler, Elsa 104

Goldwyn, Sam (Goldwynisms) 151

Grammar 128

Grinder 49

Guidelines 19

Hall, Stephen S. 76

Happiness 181, 199

Hardin, Garret 83

Hate 150

Healing 52

Heisenberg 62

Help 193-194

Heraclitus 61

Hesford, Crispin 154-155

Hopi 129

How 183

Human engineering 186

Human potential 94

Human(s) 27, 171

Hunting accidents 72, 95

Hyphens 56, 136, 170, 175, 196

Hypotheses 71

I.Q. test 161

Idealism 181

Idealization 163

Identification 95-98, 171
Identity 130, 133, 136-139, 160
IFD disease 163, 181–182
Immunotransmitters 51
Impossible 71
Indeterminate 122, 168, 170
Indexing 170-173, 179, 181, 195
Individuality 193
Indo-European languages 74, 130
Inference level(s) 25, 26, 91, 93
Inference(s) 25, 32, 70, 113-115
Influences 48
Information 114
Institute of General Semantics 18, 204, 205
Intellect 46
Intensional
    behavior 98
    definition 160
    orientations 98, 160
International Society for General Semantics 18, 204, 205
Inuit (Eskimo) 128
Is of identity 137, 179
Is of predication 138, 179
Jargon 129
Johnson, Kenneth 67, 116, 168, 196
Johnson, Wendell 17, 40, 82, 143, 163
Kendig, M. 189, 205
Keyes, Kenneth 172
Keyser, Cassius 35, 79, 203
Knots 153, 156
Know-it-all 189, 196

Knowledge 32, 63, 79, 86, 187
    current 24
    circularity of 69, 94
Know 115
Korzybski, Alfred 17, 22, 24, 27, 31, 32, 33, 35, 37, 43, 49, 56, 67, 78, 79, 81, 89, 92, 94, 102, 104, 109, 113, 116, 128, 132-133, 134, 136, 149, 151, 155, 156, 157, 161, 167-168, 174, 175, 176, 178, 202-211
Korzybska, Mira Edgerly 203
Label(s) 25, 156, 197
Labeling 106, 142-144, 152
Laing, R. D. 153
Language (Linguistic) 23, 27, 48, 68, 74, 128-130, 135, 175, 187, 194, 172
Lateral thinking 38-40
Laws of thought 130
Learn(ing) 19, 22, 109, 143, 179
Lee, Irving J. 96, 115
Lemond, Greg 72
Level(s) 24-26, 67-69, 75, 90-94, 97, 113, 124-125, 149, 172
Liberal 171
Logic 128, 130
Logical
    fate 33-35, 155
    thought 97
Love 150, 194
Macroscopic world 60
Manhood of Humanity 203, 208-9
Map(s), Mapping 48, 76-79, 86-87, 90, 92-93, 98, 146, 187
    silent level 149
Mathematics 35, 80, 203, 204, 209

Mayper, Irene Ross 179, 191
Mayper, Stuart 42, 122
McDougall, William 207
Meaning(s) 47, 48, 123, 147-151, 165, 169, 194
Measuring 62
Mental activities 97
Metaphysics 34
Meta-system 155
Micro-climate 48
Micro-culture 54, 57
Mind 46, 97, 175
Models 87
Moore, Homer J. 61
Mordkowitz, Jeffrey A. 47, 205
Movement 106, 162
Multi-'meaning' 147-149
Multi-dimensional order 84
Multi-valued orientation 140-141
Multidimensional 141
Multiordinality 149-155, 172
Murray, Elwood 205
Naming 142
Nathan, Peter W. 97
Native American Indians 143
Negotiation 191
Nelson, Thomas E. 72, 90, 97
Nerve fibers 65
Nervous system 50-52, 65, 90
Neuro-linguistic 49, 55, 65
    environments 49, 161
    factors 49
    feedback loop 69, 94, 152-153, 189
    programming (NLP) 49

Neuro-linguistics 112
Neuro-evaluational 49, 51, 55, 65, 161
Neurons 65-66
Neuroscientists 65
Neurotransmitters 51, 66
Newtonian system 37
Nierenberg, Juliet 191
Nine dot problem 44, 154
Non-additivity 83-86, 178
Non-allness 79,133, 139,182-183, 189
    terms 176-177
Non-aristotelian
    orientation 132-134
    system 38
Non-elementalism 135-136
Non-euclidian system 37
Non-identity 78, 134, 139, 160
Non-linear 84
Non-newtonian system 37, 38
Non-verbal 46, 56, 68, 69, 75, 90, 92, 100, 139, 171, 175, 181, 187, 189, 194
Nonsense 43
Object level 25, 26, 60, 90, 91, 92
    See also Silent (object) level
Observations 35, 40
Observer-observed continuum 62
Observers 62
Open systems 153-155
Operational definitions 159
Order 48, 54, 75-76, 79, 84, 92, 97, 98, 152, 158, 172, 195
Organism-as-a-whole(in-environments) 47, 50-52, 63, 107,

137, 141, 175

Orientation(s) 17, 18, 34, 130-134, 196, 201

    extensional 160, 183

    fact-finding 189

    intensional 160

    multi-valued 140-141

    two-valued 140-141

Over-defined terms 168

Paradoxes 71, 150-151

Pasteur 31

Perception(s) 70-72, 90, 97, 149

Perceptual bets 70

Perfectionism 163, 181, 197

Physico-mathematical methods 80, 204

Physiology 50, 75

Pi 77

Pictures 103

Placebo 52

Plants 27, 48

PMI method 39, 44

Po 39-40

Popper, Karl 41-42

Posture 102, 108-109

Posture-Movement 18, 162

Predictability 77, 98

Prejudging 96

Prejudice 150

Premises 32, 130-134, 192

Pre-modern-scientific 131

Prevention 199

Probability 116

Problem-solvers 155, 176

Process level 24, 26, 90, 91

Process of abstracting 67

Process(es) 24, 26, 41, 43, 60, 62, 63

Proof 41, 42, 119

Proton 60

Psycho-biological 175

Pula, Robert 60, 69, 205

Qualifying 177-178

Quantifying 177-178

Quark 60

Questioning 32

Question(s) 182-183, 193, 195

Quotes 56, 136, 170, 175, 196

Rap music 176-177

Rational Emotive Behavior Therapy (REBT) 14-15, 17, 163

Reactions to Reactions 69, 151-153, 172

Read, Allen Walker 180-181

Read, Charlotte Schuchardt 102, 104, 205

Reality 63

Real 194

Relations 54, 75, 80, 158, 187

    asymmetrical 75-76

    symmetrical 75

Relationships 192

Responsibility-taking 188-189, 191

Revising 32

Right 122, 158

Ristad, Eloise 109

Roosevelt, Franklin D. 153

Rosen, Sidney 119

Rossi, Ernest 51

Russell, Bertrand 55, 74

Safety devices 175

Sane 28

Sapir, Edward 128

Science 32, 41, 82

Science and Sanity 17. 18, 19, 186, 205

Scientific attitude 40-41, 42, 80, 155, 161, 200

Scientific method 35, 38, 187

Selfishness 210-211

Self-fulfilling prophesies 153

Self-reflexive mapping 149

Self-reflexiveness 79, 93, 146-147, 151, 189

Selver, Charlotte 104

Semantic (evaluational) reactions 46

Semantic (evaluational) relaxation 104

Semantics 23

Semmelweis 31

"Sensory awareness" 104

Sensory nerve cell 66

Shakespeare 68

Sheldon, Christopher 205

Shilts, Randy 142

Shock 72

Shoulds 197

Silence 101

Silent (object) level 25, 68, 101, 109, 110, 112-113, 194

    mapping 149

    See also Non-verbal

Similarities 137

Similarity of structure 77-79, 136

Skiers 129

Snake steaks 96

Snow 128-129

Social knowledge 32

Sombunall 177

Space-binders 27

Space-time 37, 175

Space 37

Statement(s) 92

Stockdale, Steve 205

Stomachs 164

Strate, Lance 205

Structural differential 24, 91, 204

Structure(s) 48, 54, 75, 79, 87, 102-103, 128-130, 136, 158, 176, 181

    and knowledge 76

Stupid 98, 156

Stuttering 143

Sub-atomic levels 60

Subject-predicate 74, 97, 129

Submicroscopic level 60, 132, 137

Success 163, 181-182

Survival

    in 'space' 190

    in 'time' 190, 197

    of the fittest 190

Symmetrical relations 75

Synapses 66

Syntax 97

Systems

    closed 154

    open 153, 155

Talk 23, 25

    about talking 25, 49, 79

Technology 32

Tentative forever 41-42

Terms 75, 80, 92, 147, 150, 158, 168, 181

Territory 48
    See also Map(s), Mapping

Testing 35, 40

Theory(ies) 25
    of relativity 62

Therapy 20

Think(ing) 35
    creatically 125, 155
    lateral 38-40
    verbally 102
    vertical 38-39

Time-binders 27

Time-binding 27, 32, 64, 103, 110, 186-188, 190, 193, 203, 204, 208-211
    personal 197

Time-Binding: The General Theory 186

Time-Bindings (IGS Newsletter) 18, 19, 205

Time 37

Transactions 46-47

True 122

Truish 122

Truth 97

Two-valued orientation 140-141

Un-sane 28

Uncertainty 20, 115-116
    general principle of 43
    principle 62

Uncommon sense 29, 31

Unconscious assumptions 33

Undefined terms 158

Under-defined terms 168

Unicorn 23, 27-28, 29

Unspeakable level 158

Unspeakable 101

Upset 153

Variables 80, 168, 178

Velveeta 96

Verbal behavior 46, 69
    definitions 151, 158, 160, 168-169
    level(s) 24-26, 92-94, 142, 149

Visualization 102-103, 176

Vitamin D 178

Voodoo 52

Waddington, C. H. 161

Watts, Alan 95

Weinberg, Harry 169, 188

Welles, Orson 207

What 183, 195

When 183, 195

Where 183, 195

About the Authors

Bruce I. Kodish, PhD and Susan Presby Kodish, PhD, in 1998, received the Institute of General Semantics' prestigious J. Talbot Winchell Award. With "deep appreciation and warm thanks", the award acknowledged the Kodishes' "... many contributions severally and together to the wider understanding of general semantics as authors, editors, teachers, leaders", and "their concern with the alleviation of social and individual problems, and their active interest in the on-going work in general semantics".

They together bring many years of experience in psychology, physical therapy/movement education, and GS scholarship, practice, and teaching to their writing and their individual and group work.

Susan also has edited the book *Developing Sanity in Human Affairs.*

Bruce also has written *Korzybski: A Biography*; *Dare to Inquire: Sanity and Survival for the 21st Century and Beyond*; and *Back Pain Solutions: How to Help Yourself with Posture-Movement Therapy and Education.*

Bruce and Susan's goal is to help create a safer, saner world—one person at a time.

You can learn more about their work and find GS-related links by visiting their website *www.driveyourselfsane.com* .

Printed in the USA
CPSIA information can be obtained
at www.ICGtesting.com
LVHW012341051223
765756LV00001B/109